# Safe Houses of Hope And Prayer

*Your Practical Guide To Organic Church In Your House*

Revised & Updated

By R. Maurice Smith

RISING
RIVER
MEDIA

2014 Revised Edition

Published by Rising River Media, P. O. Box 9133, Spokane, Washington 99209

**www.risingrivermedia.org**

Cover design & original art work by Gale A. Smith.
Cover photo and inside art licensed through istock.

ISBN 13       978-0-9960096-3-8

# Other Titles Available From Rising River Media

**All Dogs Go To Heaven, Don't They?**
*Biblical Reflections On Christian Universalism and Ultimate Reconciliation*

**And They Dreamt Of A Kingdom**
*Biblical Reflections On Discipleship And The Kingdom Of God - Volume 1*

**Preparing For The Coming Spiritual Outpouring**
*Reflections On The Coming Move of God's Spirit*

**River Houses Rising**
*The Rise of Safe Houses Of Hope And Prayer*

**The Least of These**
*The Role of Good Deeds In A Jesus-Shaped Spirituality*

**The Inextinguishable Blaze**
*God's Call To Holiness, Repentance, Intimacy and Spiritual Awakening*

**When Jesus Visits His Church**
*A Study Of The Seven Churches of Asia (Revelation Chapters 2-3)*

**You Wanna Do What In Your House?!**
*Straight Answers To Your Most Frequently Asked Questions About House Church*

All these titles are available on our website at *www.risingrivermedia.org* through Amazon.com!

# Table of Contents

# Author's Preface

**To The Revised Edition**

Welcome to this revised and updated edition of **Safe Houses Of Hope And Prayer**. As in the original edition, this revised and updated edition represents a continuation of my earlier book, **River Houses Rising**. Together, these two books embody my introduction to the concept of organic house church, based on more than a decade of personal experience. This revised edition has given me the opportunity to perform several housekeeping tasks which inevitably arise with any printed work. First, it has given me the opportunity to clean up inevitable typos and miscellaneous mistakes, the "little foxes" which irritate every author and editor and tend to spoil every finished work. Second, it has allowed me to clarify several concepts which were less than clear in the original edition. Third, I have taken advantage of the opportunity to add (or update) several much needed footnotes, to add a couple of Chapters of new material, and to connect the concepts expressed in this book with their more complete development in later books.

But, finally, and more importantly, this revision has offered me the opportunity to reflect both on the status of organic house church as a movement, and on what I believe God is doing in our day. If you feel sufficiently teased, you will find most of those reflections summarized in Chapter 17.

And the journey continues . . .

# Introduction

Welcome to the second installment of our *Safe Houses of Hope and Prayer* series of books on what God is doing today in and through organic house churches. This book is a continuation of the conversation we began in our earlier book, **River Houses Rising**. You will be at somewhat of a disadvantage if you have not already read that book, so I would encourage you to do so. The present book will make a lot more sense if you have read that book, especially when we refer back to key principles we discussed in detail there, but do not have the time to repeat here (principles like the difference between a religion-shaped spirituality and a Jesus-shaped spirituality). For our part we will proceed on the assumption that you are familiar with that book.

In our previous book we laid down what we believe to be some of the basic foundations for a spiritual revolution, NOT a religious reorganization. Organic house church, what we refer to as *Safe Houses of Hope and Prayer,* is NOT a re-organization of your current religious church activities - a movement from big religious boxes to smaller religious boxes (what we fondly refer to as *"Honey, I Shrunk The Church"*). *Safe Houses of Hope And Prayer* is NOT another religious program of Christian activities designed to give bored believers something to do and get excited about, and then to abandon when they get bored and the marketing campaign wears off (*"40 Days Of Purpose Driven Whatever . . . followed by eleven months of boredom"*).

# Safe Houses of Hope And Prayer

## The Greatest Challenge to the Church

The greatest challenge to the Church in any age is NOT to create programs which will attract the masses. Rather, the greatest challenge to the Church in our day is to discover what God is doing and to follow. The old theologians used to say that God is prevenient. Simply put, this means that God always acts first. It also means that we are to be a responsive people. God initiates and we respond. How we respond to what God is doing determines our usefulness and effectiveness for our generation. Organic house church, *Safe Houses of Hope and Prayer,* represents our attempt to keep pace with what God is already doing in our generation. *Safe Houses of Hope and Prayer* is our practical answer to a simple but profound question: *"How do we as believers prepare for and respond to what God wants to do in our generation?"*

Our hope is that by learning from the teachings of Scripture as well as from the past mistakes of the Church during previous times of historic revival, we can begin to respond to God's promptings today and to

> *"the greatest challenge to the Church in our day is to discover what God is doing and to follow."*

prepare for the coming move of His Spirit by asking and answering new questions. For example, if you knew that God was going to soon sweep tens of thousands of new believers into the Kingdom of God, where would you put them? Who

# Introduction

would disciple them? What would you teach them? [1]

Or if you knew that Jesus was going to visit your organic house church, what would you do to prepare? Would you spend more time in prayer seeking the Lord? Would you spend more time fasting as an act of personal repentance and sacrificial worship? Would you spend time examining your own life and the life of your Church? And are there things that Jesus might be looking for that you should pay special attention to as you prepare for His visitation? [2]

## A Church In Search of A Mission?

Some people seem to think that God has an idle church in need of something to do, a mission. To such people the news that their lives should be "purpose driven" comes as a surprise and a revelation. But the biblical truth is that God already has a mission, the same mission that sent Jesus to earth the first time. But He is in search of a church that is willing to follow and obey Him. *God's Church doesn't need a mission. God's mission needs an obedient Church.* The goal

---

[1]One historical answer to this question is found in the example of John Wesley and the Evangelical Awaking in England, which we will examine in Chapter 3. We address the issue of what to teach young disciples in our book, **And They Dreamt of A Kingdom: Biblical Reflections On Discipleship And The Kingdom of God - Volume 1**, available on our website from Amazon.com

[2]We answer this question in detail in two of our books: **When Jesus Visits His Church: A Study Of The Seven Churches of Asia (Revelation Chapters 2-3)**, and **The Inextinguishable Blaze: God's Call To Holiness, Repentance, Intimacy and Spiritual Awakening**, available on our website from Amazon.com.

# Safe Houses of Hope And Prayer

of *Safe Houses of Hope and Prayer* is to become an organic church responding in obedience to God's mission in our generation.

Our generation is witnessing profound, if not historic, spiritual changes which are confronting the Church of Jesus with new spiritual realities and new personal challenges of how to

> *"God's Church doesn't need a mission. God's mission needs an obedient Church."*

respond. Many people will look at these changes like religious square pegs staring at spiritual round holes, hoping against hope that the hole will somehow adjust itself to accommodate them unchanged. People who walk in religion-shaped spiritualities often do not adjust well to new spiritual realities. That's where many professing believers find themselves today as this new move of God unfolds.

## A Distant Mirror

History is often a mirror in which we see our own reflections in the faces and lives of those who have walked a similar path. That's why I've included a couple of stories from church history. The first is the story of Samuel and Susanna Wesley. When the Spirit of God began to move in Samuel's ministry it pushed his religion-shaped spirituality close to its breaking point. Samuel Wesley was a religious square peg staring at a spiritual round hole, unable to understand or adjust by letting go of his religion-shaped spirituality. That incident left us with a lesson that we all need to learn. You'll find it in Chapter 2.

# Introduction

History offers up another mirror for our potential benefit in the story of Samuel Wesley's son, John Wesley. Here we learn a similar lesson with a very different outcome. In the story of John Wesley we have an example of what happens when the Holy Spirit chooses to go around existing religious structures in search of new channels through which to flow. John Wesley began his religious career as a *"high churchman"* ordained in the Church of England. His religion-shaped spirituality was so strong that, looking back on his days as a religious square peg, Wesley later confessed to doubting whether a person could even be saved unless it was inside the four walls of a Church.

There were many religious square pegs in Wesley's day who stared at the spiritual round holes of Revival in stunned disbelief, unable to comprehend that the Spirit of God would choose to flow through such unlikely channels.

*"People who walk in religion-shaped spiritualities often do not adjust well to new spiritual realities."*

Religious square pegs often face a genuine spiritual crisis when God confronts them with the reality of a spiritual round hole such as an outside-the-box spiritual awakening. But history records that the Holy Spirit did, indeed, flow and therein lies a lesson for us today as we prepare for the coming spiritual outpouring. We'll unfold this story and this lesson in Chapter 3.

## Not A "How To" Book

By now it should be obvious that if you are looking for

another *"How To"* book on organic house church, this really isn't it. I don't mean to offend you, but people walking in a religion-shaped spirituality typically want *"A Ten Step 'How To' Guide To A Successful Whatever."* And unfortunately, there are always people out there willing to sell to that perceived need. But the quest for such a *"How To"* guide reveals some fundamental mis-understandings regarding the nature of organic house church and *Safe Houses of Hope And Prayer* (which may be the result of having NOT read our earlier book, **River Houses Rising**).

For example, the request for a *"How To"* guide could be based on the false assumption that all pegs are both spiritual and round and that there are no religious square pegs in need of a fundamental spiritual transformation. There are only religious round pegs in need of proper instruction on the correct structure and technique of this *"organic house church thing."*

In addition, questions regarding a *"How To"* guide may assume that the change to organic house church is simply a matter of changing structures, rather than a fundamental change in values from a religion-shaped spirituality to a Jesus-shaped spirituality. But that would be wrong,

> *"If you try to change a behavior or a structure ('going to church') before you change a value ('being the Church') the result will nearly always be a frustrated square peg and a failed house church experience."*

too. If you try to change a behavior or a structure (*"going to*

# Introduction

*church"*) before you change a value (*"being the Church"*) the result will nearly always be a frustrated square peg and a failed house church experience (*"It just didn't work out for me/us"*).

This need for a fundamental change in values from a religion-shaped spirituality to a Jesus-shaped spirituality (see Chapter 8 of **River Houses Rising**) is why I have included the Chapter entitled *"Honey, I Shrunk The Church!"* This Chapter is all about spiritual detoxing and shedding spiritual baggage. This is important because we do not want to duplicate failure by attempting to drive religious square pegs into spiritual round holes. Your journey into organic house church and *Safe Houses of Hope and Prayer* will be short and frustrating if you do not come to terms with your spiritual baggage left over from the days of your religion-shaped spirituality. Detoxing and shedding baggage functions as a two-edge sword. It weeds out the square pegs who either cannot or will not change, or it transforms them so they can successfully adjust to the new reality of spiritual round holes.

## The "Messiness" of Life and Revival

O.K., one last chapter review before we let you go to explore the rest of the book on your own. Perhaps you remember my all-time favorite movie - *Casablanca* (if not, rent a copy, pop some popcorn and enjoy one of the best movies ever made). In one scene, when the Nazis demand that Rick's *"Café Americain"* be closed, the Prefect of Police (Captain Renault, played by Claude Rains) must trump up a reason for the closure. The result is a classic scene that has become part of movie lore:

# Safe Houses of Hope And Prayer

Rick: *"How can you close me up? On what grounds?"*
Captain Renault: *"I am shocked, shocked, to find gambling going on in this establishment!"*
Emile: *"Your winnings, sir."*
Captain Renault: (in a soft voice, to Emile) *"Thank you. Thank you very much. Everybody out!"*

Harumph! Gambling in a casino? How shocking!

Some of you reading this book won't survive Chapter 4 on detoxing, but if you do, we'll catch you in Chapter 5. It's our casino-in-Casablanca moment. One of the quickest ways to spot a religion-shaped spirituality is to watch how people respond to the messiness of life, especially when it manifests in their living room. Their response is often akin to Captain Renault's, *"I am shocked, shocked, to find that there is sin in your life (as opposed to mine, which is pure as the wind-riven snow)!"* Shock and self-righteousness are frequent traveling companions in a religion-shaped spirituality.

We live in a fallen, sinful world, which is why Jesus came and died - that we might be reconciled to God and redeemed from the moral and spiritual catastrophe of our own fallenness. As a result of that cosmic catastrophe (which we call "the fall") and our own daily complicity in it, our lives are messy. The good news is that God wants to redeem the messiness of our lives and

> *"One of the quickest ways to spot a religion-shaped spirituality is to watch how people respond to 'the messiness of life,' especially when it manifests in their living room."*

# Introduction

transform us into the very image of His son. Christ-likeness is God's high calling upon each of us.

Yet, Christians continue to respond to sin and the messiness of life much like Captain Renault responded to that gambling in which he, himself, was an active participant, *"I'm shocked!"* Right. And "denial" is still a river in Egypt.

As I shared earlier, one of the quickest ways to spot a religion-shaped spirituality is to watch how people respond to the messiness of life.[3] A religion-shaped spirituality will typically respond with self-righteous shock, followed (in close and fast order) by moral outrage, judgmentalism and condemnation, a heavy dose of *"I told you so,"* and finally a discourse on *"If you would only live your life by the same ten biblical principles that I live by, this wouldn't happen, you'd be really spiritual and God would love you more."* The *coup de grâce* of this response is, of course, an invitation to a weekend seminar on *"God's Paths For Spiritual Blessing."*

Welcome to the world of religious square pegs and religion-shaped spirituality. If you find yourself in essential agreement with this approach (in other words, you're so upset with me right now that your head feels like it's going to explode), then you should probably stop reading right now. It will only get worse. Consider yourself warned!

At this point in the discussion you might conclude

---

[3]We deal with this in several examples from Jesus' ministry in our book, **And They Dreamt Of A Kingdom**. See particularly *"Lesson 35 - She Who Loves Much."*

(wrongfully) that a Jesus-shaped spirituality is somehow soft on sin. Not so. We're just lite on legalism. Like Jesus weeping at the tomb of Lazarus, a Jesus-shaped spirituality weeps at the personal destruction and death that the catastrophe of sin has brought upon the world, and how it continues to ravage the lives of those around us - both inside and outside the Church. But a Jesus-shaped spirituality understands that the catastrophe of sin and its consequences cannot be undone - even in the life of the believer - by any set of rules, principles or guidelines, masquerading as holiness, regardless of how well intended.

Genuine holiness is to legalism what a genuine $100 bill is to a counterfeit. Outwardly they resemble one another in appearance, enough so that an untrained eye might mistake one for the other. But that's where the similarities end. When the truth is exposed, one will let you shop at Walmart, while the other will send you to prison for 20 years. That genuine holiness of a Jesus-shaped spirituality, produced by a personal encounter with a burning coal fresh from God's altar, will transform the individual and enable them to obey God with a joyful heart and a clear conscience. The false

> *"Genuine holiness is to legalism what a genuine $100 bill is to a counterfeit."*

holiness of legalism and its rules will imprison you in a life of guilt, anger, frustration and self-righteousness. Legalism is the fool's gold of the domain of darkness. You can't spend it in the Kingdom of God.

A Jesus-shaped spirituality places its faith and its hope, not

# Introduction

in the outward conformity of the individual to a set of religious rules, but in the inward spiritual transformation of the individual by the Holy Spirit. And that, ultimately, is the scandal of Chapter

> *"Legalism is the fool's gold of the domain of darkness. You can't spend it in the Kingdom of God."*

5. I hope you survive it. If not, Captain Renault and I will send flowers.

## Your Invitation To "The Scandal"

And this leads me to the scandal of organic house church and *Safe Houses of Hope and Prayer*.[4] The scandal is our firm belief that Jesus wants to visit His Church and to pour out the River of His Spirit which will flow in spiritual power and blessing unknown in the experience of our generation. And in the process of that divine visitation He wants to indelibly imprint a new-but-old DNA upon her character, a DNA of genuine holiness and the fear of God, genuine personal repentance and renewed intimacy with Himself. Why? So that in the generations of house churches yet to be born we will multiply and reproduce believers and churches where repentance, intimacy and holiness are the norm, just as the prophet Zechariah foresaw:

*"And on that day there shall be inscribed on the bells of the*

---

[4]Our English word "scandal" comes from the Greek word *skandalon*, meaning *"to stumble."* The idea that God might use a vessel like organic house church for the next move of His Spirit will cause many Christians to "stumble."

*horses, 'Holy to the LORD.' And the pots in the house of the LORD shall be as the bowls before the altar. And every pot in Jerusalem and Judah shall be holy to the LORD of hosts, so that all who sacrifice may come and take of them and boil the meat of the sacrifice in them."* (Zechariah 14:20-21)

God is preparing His end-time harvest. And to accommodate that harvest He is raising up tens of thousands of multiplying organic house churches, *Safe Houses of Hope and Prayer*, led by believers just like you. These organic house churches, meeting in homes like yours and led by Kingdom-minded disciples like you, will be the new vessels for what God is doing in our day. And He is calling you to be a part of it. The only question remaining is this: *Are you ready to become a part of what God is doing in our day?*

# Chapter 1

## Your House Could Change The World

*"These men who have upset the world have come here also . . ."* (Acts 17:6)

When was the last time anyone accused you of turning your world upside down? Now that's a question that deserves some unpacking, because so many believers seem to have given up on the idea of turning their world upside down. Indeed, it is estimated that as many as 10 million people just like you have dropped out of traditional churches in America alone. Author Reggie McNeal, himself a leader among Southern Baptists, describes the situation this way:

*"A growing number of people are leaving the institutional church for a new reason. They are not leaving because they have lost faith. They are leaving the church to preserve their faith. They contend that the church no longer contributes to their spiritual development. In fact, they say, quite the opposite. The number of "post-generational" Christians is growing. David Barrett, author of the World Christian Encyclopedia, estimates that there are about 112 million "churchless Christians" world wide, and about 5 percent of all adherents, but he projects that number will double in the next twenty five years!"* [5]

---

[5]Reggie McNeal, *The Present Future: Six Tough Questions for the Church* (San Francisco: John Wiley & Sons, 2003), p. 4.

# Safe Houses of Hope And Prayer

If people have not lost their faith, then why the exodus from traditional *Churchianity*?[6] Perhaps it is because these believers feel powerless to change the world around them. Perhaps it is because they feel that the traditional institutional church they have known no longer works like it should - like they have always imagined that it could. Whatever the reason, many professing believers have not only left *Churchianity*, they have also lost any vision or sense of calling that they can (or should) change their neighborhood or their community, much less turn their world upside down! And without such a vision, people perish, and lead·silent lives of spiritual frustration and disillusionment. Does that describe you?

## Then Versus Now

Wow! How different our current day situation is from those early Christians in the New Testament book of Acts. In something like 20 years from the time of Jesus' resurrection and ascension, they were being accused by unbelievers of upsetting the whole world (literally, *"men who have thrown the inhabited earth into an uproar"*). What did they do to change their world, while we seem so powerless and ineffective in changing ours? They met together in one another's homes. They devoted themselves to each other, to teaching, to genuine biblical community (as opposed to superficial fellowship, to sharing meals together, and to prayer. They rejoiced together and suffered together. They

---

[6]*"Churchianity"* is a term officially coined by Michael Spencer, **Mere Churchianity: Finding Your Way Back To Jesus-Shaped Spirituality** (Colorado Springs: Waterbrook Press, 2010)

# Your House Could Change The World

shared their lives with one another and met one another's needs. They proclaimed the good news of the Kingdom of God together and suffered persecution together. And sometimes they even died together. They didn't simply believe the truth, they embodied the truth in a Jesus-shaped spirituality which they lived out authentically in a way that changed the world. Their homes became organic hotbeds of God's absolute truth that God's Messiah, Jesus of Nazareth, had lived, died, been raised from the dead and ascended into heaven and that God was now establishing His Kingdom and calling all men everywhere to repent and believe. Both individually and as a believing body they pursued a Jesus-shaped spirituality, and they offered a skeptical pagan (but religion-soaked) world a clear glimpse of the reality of the Kingdom of God.

## Changing The World, One House At A Time

This message that the Kingdom of God had arrived and that Jesus was Lord converted a Roman Centurian in Caesarea, won over the Roman Governor of Cyprus, confounded Greek philosophers in Athens, disturbed the religious status quo in Thessalonica, caused lawsuits in Corinth and economic riots in Ephesus. It moved quietly from one house to the next in silent triumph, transforming their homes into organic house churches and *Safe Houses of Hope and Prayer*. The homes of a Roman Centurian and a woman fabric merchant in Philippi. The home of Aquila and his wife Priscilla, Jewish-Christian refugees from Rome. The home of a Gentile God-fearer named Titius Justus and the home of Crispus, the synagogue leader in Corinth. All of these, and more, were now part of a growing silent network of homes and families conquered by the good news of the Kingdom of God and the Lordship of King Jesus. For the next 250 years these ancient networks of organic house churches, *Safe Houses of Hope And Prayer*, served as God's vessels and instruments to turn the ancient world upside down and to bring the Roman Empire to its knees.

## It's Time To Turn The World Upside Down!

In a day when traditional church attendance is declining and Christians are feeling powerless and frustrated, it should come as no surprise that God is again raising up thousands of networking organic house churches! We call them *Safe Houses of Hope And Prayer*. Like those ancient believers in the book of Acts, I believe that it is once again time for believers to turn our world upside down with *Safe Houses of Hope And Prayer*, organic house churches meeting in homes just like yours. We're looking for people of peace who want their homes to become *Safe Houses of Hope And Prayer*. Are you ready for the Kingdom of God to come to your house? Are you ready to turn your world upside down?

## Making This Personal

Organic house church and *Safe Houses of Hope and Prayer* represent God's call to spiritual adventure in the Kingdom of God and personal greatness in your generation. What about you? What is your personal vision for how God might use you to change your world?

# Chapter 2

## Samuel Wesley Had A Swimming Pool
*(And Why It Matters!)*

When it comes to turning our world upside down for the Kingdom of God, we need to ask ourselves a basic question: *"What is God doing, and how can we participate?"* If God really is prevenient - He initiates and we respond - then what is He initiating that we need to respond to? Failure to ask that question and to answer it correctly will leave us as square pegs in search of round holes. And that really is frustrating.

To apply this question more specifically to church we need to ask ourselves: *"What expression of church is God raising up in our generation as the channel to receive the coming outpouring of His Spirit as it flows in fresh power in spiritual awakening and revival?"*

Both Scripture and the history of the Church teach us that God is always looking for channels through which the River of His Spirit can flow. But men tend to want to build swimming pools where they can siphon off and capture a portion of the River of God's Spirit, appoint lifeguards to watch over the swimmers who come, offer swimming classes, hold "Holy

> *"When it comes to turning our world upside down for the Kingdom of God, we need to ask ourselves a basic question: 'What is God doing, and how can we participate?'"*

# Safe Houses of Hope And Prayer

Spirit pool parties," create committees to decide whether or not to build a bigger swimming pool, and what rules they should establish to rule and control what actually belongs to God.

In seasons of spiritual awakening the River of God's Spirit begins to flow. Old channels through which the River may have flowed in times past, but which have since become dammed up by unbelief, control and religion are by-passed as the River seeks new channels where it can flow freely. Want proof that this is true? Just ask Samuel Wesley. Better yet, ask his wife Susanna.

If you don't recognize the names of Samuel and Susanna Wesley, then perhaps you'll recognize the names of two of their sons, John and Charles Wesley. If not, don't worry. You soon will.

In the early 1700s Samuel Wesley was the Anglican (Church of England) Rector of St. Andrew's Church in, Epworth, Lincolnshire, England. Samuel served as Rector there after the family moved to Epworth in 1695. It was in that Rectory at Epworth (which you can still visit today) that Samuel and his wife, Susanna, raised their family of seven children (nineteen were born, but only seven lived) and where Samuel served as Rector (pastor) of the parish church until his death in 1735.

## The "Scandal"

In the winter of 1711-12 Samuel was called away to London on Church business for several months. In his absence

# Samuel Wesley Had A Swimming Pool

Samuel arranged for a fellow pastor - one Reverend Inman - to preach and minister in his place (in other words, to supervise the swimming pool) until he could return.

That was a mistake. The man had little or no preaching ability, and people liked the man even less than they liked his sermons. When friends and neighbors and members of the congregation learned that Susanna was holding devotions for her children at their home on Sunday evening they began asking to attend. Soon, there were forty people attending Susanna's Sunday evening devotionals. Susanna would read prayers, one of Samuel's sermons and then devotional topics would be discussed. Soon the crowd of 40 had grown to over 200 people crowding into the small rectory on Sunday evening to hear Susanna read Samuel's sermons and discus devotional topics. A house church of considerable size had been born outside of the official swimming pool of the church. And that was a scandal.

The Reverend Inman took great offense at such a scandal. People were neglecting the Sunday morning services and attending Susanna's evening meeting instead. Irate, Reverend Inman wrote to Samuel in London and complained. Samuel wrote to his wife, expressing his concern that she should be supporting the interim preacher. He encouraged her to discontinue these evening meetings.

## The Response

Samuel offered three basic objections to what was going on. *First,* he objected that the Sunday evening meetings will look *"particular"* (i.e., peculiar, strange). **Second,** he reminded

# Safe Houses of Hope And Prayer

Susanna that she was a woman and, therefore, should not be leading such meetings. **Third,** Samuel reminded Susanna that he had a *"public station"* to protect.

But Susanna Wesley was not a woman easily deterred from what she believed to be God's will. She wrote back to Samuel and addressed his concerns. **First,** she reminded her husband that in *"our corrupt age"* the genuine work of God will always look peculiar. **Second**, as to her being a woman, she reminded Samuel that in addition to being a woman she was also the "mistress of a large family" which he, in his absence, had entrusted to her care. The evening family devotions were simply part of her attempt to see to the spiritual condition of their children. The fact that the children had told their friends who had told their parents, and that those parents now asked permission to attend the meetings, was not her fault.

*"But I never did positively presume to hope that God would make use of me as an instrument in doing good; the farthest I ever did go was, 'It may be: who can tell? With God all things are possible.' I will resign myself to him; or as Herbert better expresses it,*

> *Only, since God doth often vessels make*
> *Of lowly matter, for high uses meet,*
> *I throw me at His feet;*
> *There will I lie until my Maker seek*
> *For some mean stuff whereon to show His skill;*
> *Then is my time.*

# Samuel Wesley Had A Swimming Pool

When Samuel raised new objections in another letter and expressed his desire that she discontinue the meetings, Susanna wrote back and told him that she would reluctantly stop the meetings, but only if he specifically instructed her to do so:

> *"(Susanna) reminded her husband that in 'our corrupt age' the genuine work of God will always look peculiar."*

*"If you do after all think fit to dissolve this assembly, do not tell me any more that you desire me to do it, for that will not satisfy my conscience; but send me your positive command in such full and express terms as may absolve me from all guilt and punishment for neglecting this opportunity of doing good to souls, when you and I shall appear before the great and awful tribunal of our Lord Jesus Christ."*

Wow! Can you imagine arguing with this woman?! No letter containing such instructions ever arrived. Samuel's eventual return home from London brought an end to this extraordinary house church meeting in the Epworth Rectory. The crowds scattered, without returning to the parish church. And life at the church swimming pool returned to normal.[7]

## What Could Have Been (But Never Was)

Samuel Wesley was a religious square peg who had been

---

[7]One could say that the Kingdom grew, but not the church. Our account of these events is taken from Charles Wallace (Editor), **Susanna Wesley: The Complete Writings** (Oxford University Press US, 1997). See specifically Chapter 5, *"The Evening Prayers Controversy"*

confronted with a spiritual round hole, and no amount of pounding by his godly wife could ever make the two fit. His religion-shaped spirituality saw the Church and the Kingdom of God as a public swimming pool to be managed by properly trained and appointed caretakers, regardless of their skill or gifting. And

*"A religion-shaped spirituality sees the Church and the Kingdom as a public swimming pool to be managed by properly trained and appointed caretakers, regardless of their skill or gifting."*

because a religion-shaped spirituality tends to leave people somewhat myopic, he hadn't seen or noticed that the River of God had, for a brief time, flowed through his own home in great power. That's the problem with church swimming pools and their caretakers. They tend to view the River of God's Spirit as a threat, not a blessing. That is, if they even see it at all.

### What Can We Learn From All This?

I have included this story of Susanna and Samuel Wesley because it offers us both observations and questions which are relevant to organic house church and *Safe Houses of Hope and Prayer* today.

For example, by way of observation you could say that organic house church, such as *Safe Houses of Hope and Prayer*, is a spiritual phenomenon that has been struggling to be re-born into the life of God's people for nearly 300 years! The Preacher of Ecclesiastes was (and is) right. There really

# Samuel Wesley Had A Swimming Pool

is nothing new under the sun (Ecclesiastes 1:9)!

Now, by way of questions, this incident presents us with several questions and concerns that are re-surfacing in today's organic house church movement. Reflecting on the story of this Chapter, how would you respond to the following?

*Reflection Question # 1 -* What did you learn from the story of Samuel and Susanna Wesley? Who do you think was "right" or "wrong" in the controversy? Why?

*Reflection Question # 2 -* What are believers suppose to do when traditional institutional expressions of church no longer meet the spiritual and practical needs of those under their care; and the leadership is unwilling to take note or change.

*Reflection Question # 3 -* What are your attitudes regarding women like Susanna Wesley in leadership, including leading an organic house church?

*Reflection Question # 4 -* How do organic house churches like *Safe Houses of Hope and Prayer* look peculiar when compared with traditional institutional church ministry today? Does this bother you? Why or why not?

# Safe Houses of Hope And Prayer

*Reflection Question # 5 -* What should be our response to pastors and other  traditional leaders who feel threatened and scandalized by new organic forms of Church, including organic house churches and *Safe Houses of Hope And Prayer*.

Congratulations! You have just taken an important step in answering your own questions, and becoming an organic house church and the *Safe House of Hope and Prayer* in your house!

But, hang on! The scandal isn't over. Indeed, all of these issues, along with many more, would eventually re-surface and present fresh challenges to the Church thirty years later during the great Evangelical Awakening under the ministry of Samuel and Susanna's son, John. And that's where we want to turn our attention now.

# Chapter 3

## John Wesley Discovers House Churches

John Wesley was nine years old during the *"Evening Prayers Controversy."* We don't really know how much he knew or understood of what occurred, but in his later evangelistic career Wesley demonstrated that he was keenly aware of the shortcomings of the institutional church and the problem of attempting to drive square religious pegs into round spiritual holes.

Born in 1703, the fifteenth child of Samuel Wesley and his wife Susanna Annesley, John Wesley entered Christ Church, Oxford in 1720 as an undergraduate at the age of 17. He graduated four years later, in 1724. In March of 1726 Wesley became a *Fellow* (instructor) at Lincoln College, Oxford. The next year he left Oxford to assist his father, Samuel, in his ministerial duties at Epworth and Wroote. John was ordained a priest in the Anglican Church in 1728, and the following year Christ Church College recalled him to teach. He would remain at Oxford for the next 8 years. Along with his brother Charles (now an Undergraduate at Christ Church) and their friends William Morgan and Robert Kirkham of Merton College, John formed the *"Holy Club."* They became known among the student body for their methodical habits of personal devotions, a regular schedule of study and a dedicated commitment to social work, particularly among the inmates of Castle Prison. In 1732 students at Oxford labeled John and his associates *"Methodists"* (after their "methodical" behavior) and the name stuck.

## Safe Houses of Hope And Prayer

The morning of October 14, 1735, found John Wesley and his brother Charles leaving England aboard the sailing ship *"The Simmonds,"* bound for Savannah in the Province of Georgia in the American colonies. Governor James Oglethorpe had requested that John serve as the minister of the newly formed Savannah parish. For his part, John hoped to work as a missionary among the American Indians of Georgia. They reached Savannah on 8 February 1736. Despite some early successes, the

*"I went to America, to convert the Indians; but oh! who shall convert me?"*

experience did not go well, and in early 1738 Wesley was forced to flee Georgia and return to England under a cloud of accusations and self-doubt. On the voyage home a deeply defeated Wesley wrote in his personal journal for 24th January 1738, *"I went to America, to convert the Indians; but oh! who shall convert me?"* Wesley was a man in deep personal crisis over the shallowness of his own faith. He continued on in his journal:

*"Who, what is he that will deliver me from this evil heart of mischief? I have a fair summer religion. I can talk well; nay, and believe myself, while no danger is near; but let death look me in the face, and my spirit is troubled. [Then] I have a sin of fear, that when I've spun my last thread, I shall perish on the shore!"*

An historian of John Wesley's life once observed that if John Wesley had died at the age of 35, following his disastrous adventure in Georgia, he would have been remembered as a gifted and well intended failure. Simply put, Wesley's

# John Wesley Discovers House Churches

religion-shaped spirituality had utterly failed him, leaving him a frustrated and defeated young man, full of spiritual self-doubt.

But all of that changed on the evening of May 24, 1738 when Wesley attended a Moravian prayer meeting and experienced a profound personal encounter with God that transformed his life and ministry. Here is how Wesley himself described it:

*"In the evening I went very unwillingly to a society in Aldersgate Street, where one was reading Luther's preface to the Epistle to the Romans. About a quarter before nine, while the leader was describing the change which God works in the heart through faith in Christ, I felt my heart strangely warmed. I felt I did trust in Christ alone for salvation; and an assurance was given me that He had taken away my sins, even mine, and saved me from the law of sin and death."*

From that day forward, John Wesley was a changed man. He began letting go of his religion-shaped spirituality, leaving the four walls of the church to preach the gospel in the streets, public squares and fields of England. Tens of thousands of people came to saving faith in Christ outside the four walls of the existing religious structure. Wesley trained lay men and women to do the work of the ministry(a revolutionary innovation in his day), and he divided converts into groups of twelve (called "Classes") which met on Thursday evenings in people's homes That's right! House churches led by women. Imagine that 240 years ago! Such a radical departure from proper church protocol deserves a close look!

# Safe Houses of Hope And Prayer

## What To Do With The "Awakened"?

Wesley's Aldersgate Street experience transformed both the man and his ministry. He began to preach an evangelical message of personal salvation with a personal confidence and spiritual power he had never experienced before. When the doors of Anglican Churches and parishes closed to Wesley and his evangelical message, He began preaching in the open air fields and public squares of England. In his preaching ministry throughout the chapels, by-ways and fields of England, Wesley regarded those who responded to his gospel message as people whom the Spirit had awakened. Whether or not they were truly regenerate could only be determined over a period of time during which the individual must be given pastoral care, close examination and personal discipleship. All of these awakened respondents were invited to attend Wesley's Methodist Society meetings.

*"There is only one condition previously required of those who desire admission into these societies,"* Wesley wrote, *"a desire 'to flee from the wrath to come, and to be saved from their sins.'"* [8]

But a problem soon arose. The River of God's Spirit was beginning to flow in great power and revival. Wesley's preaching ministry was so successful that in the year 1743 alone one thousand new members were added to his London

---

[8]David Francis Holsclaw, *"The Demise of Disciplined Christian Fellowship: The Methodist Class Meeting in Nineteenth-Century America,"* A Doctoral Dissertation in History in the Graduate Division of the University of California, Davis, 1982. Page 27.

# John Wesley Discovers House Churches

Society. This kind of rapid growth presented a problem for personal pastoral care and supervision. How were so many "awakened" seekers to be discipled and encouraged? And how were false professors to be weeded out? In spite of the large numbers confonting him, Wesley was adamant concerning the need for constant, personal pastoral care. *"How grievously are they mistaken who imagine that as soon as the children are born they need take no more care of them,"* he wrote.[9] But how could he personally disciple so many people?

## The Birth of The "Class of 12"

The answer to Wesley's problem began in the city of Bristol where Wesley's Methodist Society meeting had grown to 1,100 people. A Society member by the name of Captain Foy (that's all we know about him) suggested that one person could call on eleven others during the week to check on them and see how they were doing. The suggestion was adopted and the Bristol Society was soon transformed.

> *"This kind of rapid growth presented a problem for personal pastoral care and supervision. How were so many 'awakened' seekers to be discipled and encouraged?"*

*"In a while, some [class leaders] informed me that they found such and such a one did not live as he ought. It struck me*

---

[9]Holsclaw, page 13.

*immediately, 'This is one thing, the very thing we have wanted so long.'"* [10]

These weekly visits for discipleship and pastoral care soon became weekly meetings.

*"This was the origin of our classes at London,"* Wesley wrote, *"for which I can never sufficiently praise God, the unspeakable usefulness of the institution having ever since been more and more manifest."* [11]

The structure quickly took shape. Soon, every Methodist Society was broken into smaller Classes of 12 persons who met weekly with a Class Leader for pastoral care, examination, encouragement and exhortation. It was discipleship, 18th Century Methodist style. According to Wesley,

*"Many now happily experienced that Christian fellowship of which they had not so much as an idea before. They began to 'bear one another's burdens,' and naturally to 'care for each other.' As they had daily a more intimate acquaintance with, so they had a more endeared affection for, each other."* [12]

The Wesleyan "Class," consisting of 12 people meeting together every Thursday evening in private homes to pursue

---

[10]Holsclaw, page 38.

[11]Holsclaw, page 39.

[12]Holsclaw, page 41.

# John Wesley Discovers House Churches

personal discipleship, became the centerpiece of the Methodist Church for the next 100 years. It was in the Class that spiritually awakened individuals were discipled, examined and instructed, and where they experienced biblical community and learned to bear one another's burdens. It was in the Class that the Rules (the written standards of behavior expected of every Methodist) were read and where individuals were examined to see if they were sincere in their desire to live according to Methodist discipline.

## Round Pegs and Square Holes

Like his mother thirty years earlier, John Wesley had simply looked for and found a way to overcome the on-going problem of a dysfunctional institutional church in order to meet the spiritual needs of new believers who were being swept into the Kingdom of God through the on-going revival. *The movement of God in the Evangelical Awakening was producing large numbers of newly converted "spiritual round pegs" who simply could not fit into the "religious square holes" of the existing church structure.*

The new and growing Methodist Church with its multiplying Class structure, was nothing less than a spiritual revolution - as opposed to a religious re-organization - in how to "do" church. For all practical purposes, it was an organic house church structure within the larger structure of the institutional Anglican Church. And by choosing a path of discipleship that was essentially organic, Wesley created a structure that accomplished at least four important tasks.

# Safe Houses of Hope And Prayer

**First,** he created a structure that could receive the rapidly increasing fruit of widespread revival and could offer a secure fellowship in which new converts and young believers could be nurtured and discipled.

**Second,** he created a structure that was flexible enough to serve as a channel for the River of God's Spirit as it flowed in power while avoiding (for many years) the temptation to create a man-made swimming pool to control what God was doing.

*"The movement of God in the Evangelical Awakening was producing large numbers of newly converted 'spiritual round pegs' who simply could not fit into the 'religious square holes' of the existing church structure."*

**Third,** he created a persecution resistant structure that successfully withstood the sporadic and sometimes intense persecution that Methodists experienced at the hands of the institutional church (there are documented stories of Methodist leaders' homes being ransacked and burned by angry crowds while local officials stood by and watched).

**Fourth,** he created a structure with a DNA of sacrificial service to *"the least of these."* One of the weekly tasks of the Class Leader was to collect the weekly "penny tax." Each week every Methodist was required to pay one penny (a lot more money then than now!) into a fund that was used exclusively to minister to the poor of the city.

# John Wesley Discovers House Churches

## The Old Becomes New - Again!

It is an unfortunate reality of history that, within 50 years of Wesley's death (in 1791) the Methodist Class structure began to break down into institutional Church swimming pools. As Methodism built their own dedicated buildings, the meetings were moved from private homes to those buildings, the Classes subsequently grew in size under popular leaders, and religious swimming pools were born again.

But the old is about to become new again. New times of spiritual outpouring and awakening, along with new challenges are now confronting old dysfunctionalities to demand new wineskins such as organic house church and *Safe Houses of Hope and Prayer*. It happened to Susanna Wesley, and thirty years later to her son, John. And it is happening again today. In His sovereign Providence, God is raising up organic house churches as His new-but-old wineskin for spiritual renewal and awakening. How successful we will ultimately be will depend in no small part on how well we learn the lessons of the past without repeating their mistakes.

## What Can We Learn?

So, what can we learn from Wesley's experience that is relevant to organic house church and *Safe Houses of Hope and Prayer* today? Let's ask ourselves some questions:

***Reflection Question #1 -*** What stood out to you from this story? What specifically did you learn that you will take away and chew on for a while?

*Reflection Question #2* - Based on what you have seen so far, what is the difference between a spiritual revolution and a religious re-organization? In your opinion, what did John Wesley do that was revolutionary?

*Reflection Question #3* - How difficult do you think it was for Wesley and others of his day to make the transition from the religion-shaped spirituality of "high church" Anglicanism, to the Jesus-shaped spirituality of preaching in public squares and meeting in small house church groups?

And this leads us to the personal issue of spiritual detoxing and *"Honey, I Shrunk The Church."*

# Chapter 4

## Honey, I Shrunk The Church!

O.K., let's begin this chapter with a story I like to call *"Die Heretic!"* It goes like this. Once I saw this guy on a bridge about to jump.

I said, *"Don't do it!"*

He said, *"Nobody loves me."*

I said, *"God loves you. Do you believe in God?"*

He said, *"Yes."*

I said, *"Are you a Christian or a Jew?"*

He said, *"A Christian."*

I said, *"Me, too! Protestant or Catholic?"*

He said, *"Protestant."*

I said, *"Me, too! What franchise?"*

He said, *"Baptist."*

I said, *"Me, too! Northern Baptist or Southern Baptist?"*

He said, *"Northern Baptist."*

I said, *"Me, too! Northern Conservative Baptist or Northern Liberal Baptist?"*

He said, *"Northern Conservative Baptist."*

I said, *"Me, too! Northern Conservative Baptist Great Lakes Region, or Northern Conservative Baptist Eastern Region?"*

He said, *"Northern Conservative Baptist Great Lakes Region."*

I said, *"Me, too! Northern Conservative Baptist Great Lakes Region Council of 1879, or Northern Conservative Baptist Great Lakes Region Council of 1912?"*

He said, *"Northern Conservative Baptist Great Lakes Region Council of 1912."*

So, I said, *"Die, heretic!"* And I pushed him over.

## Safe Houses of Hope And Prayer

O.K., if you're having trouble with the punch line then you're a little slower than I had hoped, but let me help you out (as opposed to pushing you over). The story makes a sad (but funny!) point, namely, that Christians seem to love to fight over things that few people understand or care about. In terms of our on-going discussion regarding organic house church and *Safe Houses of Hope and Prayer*, it poses a fundamental question that we must address: *Does that represent the kind of religion-shaped spirituality that you want in your house church?* This is important because a religion-shaped spirituality will seek to reproduce whatever religious structure produced it in the first place. And religious square pegs simply will not fit into spiritual round holes, regardless of how hard you pound (and why would you even want to?). Indeed, if you try to move a religious square peg from a large peg board to a smaller one, the end result will inevitably be a phenomenon we like to call, *"Honey, I Shrunk The Church."* [13]

### Careful There With That Shrinking Ray!

If you have kids, then you have probably seen the 1989 comedy movie, *"Honey, I Shrunk the Kids."* In the film Rick Moranis (whom I loved in *"Ghost Busters"*) stars as Wayne Szalinski, an eccentric professor and inventor who accidentally shrinks his kids, along with his neighbor's kids, to one-quarter (1/4) of an inch with his electro-magnetic

---

[13]It is estimated that there are at least 38,000 Christian denominations. If anyone ever asks you, *"Why are there so many denominations?"* feel free to share the story of *"Die Heretic"* with them. It makes about as much sense as any other explanation you can give. People fight and split over the darndest things.

# Honey, I Shrunk The Church!

shrink ray and inadvertently sweeps them out into the backyard with the trash. (Yeah, I know, happens to me all the time, too!).

Unable to resist the apparently overwhelming urge to mimic a good line, someone in the organic house church movement coined the phrase, *"Honey, I Shrunk The Church!"* We all groaned when we first heard it because we realized it adequately describes the all-too-human tendency of people to take what they know from traditional institutional church and simply shrink it down to fit into their living room or basement. The temptation is to bring our religion-shaped spirituality with its failed models, bad behavior and incompatible values into organic house church.

Having witnessed it too many times to be a coincidence, I'm convinced that somewhere in a Church basement, Wayne Szalinski is busy at work, shrinking traditional churches and religion-shaped spiritualities to a size small enough to fit into an average sized living room (I've even seen them complete with miniature pulpit and organ)! Once that process is underway, it isn't long before organic house churches stop being organic and growing, and start splitting as another *"Die Heretic"* story unfolds in someone's living room.

> *"The temptation is to bring our religion-shaped spirituality with its failed models, bad behavior and incompatible values into organic house church."*

# Safe Houses of Hope And Prayer

## Detox Before Flossing!

We live in a generation where people spend more time flossing and caring for their teeth than they spend caring for their spiritual condition (O.K., I had to work the whole flossing thing in there somehow!).

People will spend more time in front of a mirror flossing and examining their dental work than they will spend examining their spiritual or religious values to see if they are genuine, biblical or even godly. And, yes, that includes many professing Christians. This struggle between competing values is highlighted in the chart on the following page.

> *"We live in a generation where people spend more time flossing and caring for their teeth than they spend caring for their spiritual condition."*

Someone once observed that we start out by shaping our buildings, but in the end our buildings shape us. Many professing Christians began their spiritual journeys into the Kingdom in the genuine pursuit of a Jesus-shaped spirituality. But somewhere in the process they allowed the buildings - the structures - of institutional *Churchianity* to warp their values to reflect the values of the building. Somewhere along the way their Jesus-shaped spirituality was replaced with a religion-shaped spirituality. They began by shaping their building, but now their building has shaped them.

# Honey, I Shrunk The Church!

| Comparing Values | |
|---|---|
| **Organic House Church** | **Institutional Churches** |
| Be the Church | Go to Church |
| Church is simple | Church is complex |
| Jesus-Shaped Spirituality | Religion-Shaped Spirituality |
| Church As Organism | Church As Organization |
| Meets around people | Meets around facility and day |
| Church as people & mission | Church as institution & program |
| Low Maintenance | High Maintenance |
| Discipleship by modeling | Discipleship by instruction |
| Equip believers for ministry | Preach & administer programs |
| Leadership by gift | Leadership by office/position |
| Meet needs, equip people | Maintain organization |
| Do missions | Give to missions |
| Genuine Community | Pseudo-Community |
| Leaders gifted & anointed | Leaders elected or appointed |
| Persecution resistant | Persecution vulnerable |
| What Would Jesus Do? | What Are Leaders Doing? |
| The Kingdom of God | The Organization |

## Baggage Check

When I was in seminary in the early 1980s in Denver, plans were announced by the regional government to replace the existing Stapleton Airport with a new regional airport outside of the City. It took twenty years of planning and building for the new Denver International Airport (DIA) to

*"Physical baggage is often a metaphor for spiritual baggage."*

become a reality. As the day approached for the Grand Opening of the new airport there was a glitch. The airport authority had spent literally hundreds of millions of dollars on a new computerized and automated system to handle passenger baggage. The trouble was that it didn't work. The opening of the new multi-billion airport facility had to be delayed because it couldn't handle people's baggage. Welcome to the Church. Our baggage handling system doesn't work very well either and needs to be fixed.

In Matthew 10:9-10 Jesus talked to His disciples about the importance of shedding baggage and traveling light. Listen to what he said: *"Do not acquire gold, or silver, or copper for your money belts, or a bag for your journey, or even two tunics, or sandals, or a staff; for the worker is worthy of his support."* (NASB)

Physical baggage is often a metaphor for spiritual baggage. Just as Jesus instructed the disciples to travel light by shedding physical baggage, so too we need to help one another to travel lite by shedding religious baggage which will slow us down from what God is calling us to do. How much time do you want to spend as a religious square peg trying to pound yourself into a spiritual round hole?

The problem of religious baggage and square pegs is really nothing new. In fact, it is a timeless phenomenon. Religious

# Honey, I Shrunk The Church!

square pegs and their religious baggage created a crisis in the 1$^{st}$ Century New Testament Church during the transition period leading up to Acts 15 (the Jerusalem Council). In the transition from the religion-shaped spirituality of institutional Judaism to the Jesus-shaped spirituality of early Christianity, the early church was forced to deal with (and shed) a great deal of religious baggage left over from its Jewish roots. That included shedding the 5,000 (or so) quasi-laws, called "Traditions of the Elders," which governed the daily religious life of every 1$^{st}$ Century Jew .

Religious square pegs known as Judaizers taught that Gentile (non-Jewish) believers had to be circumcised and keep the Law of Moses in order to be truly saved and spiritual. In other words, one had to become a good Jew before they could become a good Christian. The expansion of the church to the Gentiles, who neither understood nor cared about the religion-shaped spirituality of Judaism, forced the early Church and its leaders to re-think their understanding of a Jesus-shaped spirituality in order to avoid *"placing upon the neck of the disciples a yoke which neither our fathers nor we have been able to bear"* (Acts 15:10 - NASB).

Later, during his missionary journeys, the Apostle Paul was forced to confront the same religious square pegs. Writing to the young house churches of Colossae (see Colossians 2:16-18) he warned them not to allow religious baggage regarding food (Jewish dietary laws), a festival or a new moon (observing Old Testament Jewish feasts), or a Sabbath day (meeting on the Jewish Sabbath) to deter them from their pursuit of a Jesus-shaped spirituality. Paul gave the same advice (only more strongly) to the young house churches of Galatia, urging them to reject the religious baggage of Jewish legalism that those religious square peg Judiazers were attempting to impose upon the Christian community.

> *"Beware of religious baggage left over from the religion-shaped spirituality of the past."*

Finally, to his spiritual son and disciple, Timothy, Paul gave pastoral instructions on dealing with the religious baggage brought into the Church by religious square pegs in the form of false teachers promoting such things as myths, and genealogies, and mere speculations and fruitless discussions. Sometimes, religious square pegs and their religious baggage seem to come in a never ending stream of foolishness.

Beware of religious baggage left over from the religion-shaped spirituality of the past. Organic house church isn't about your view of politics, the rapture, the end-times, Pentecostal manifestations, recovering the Old Testament feasts or a host of other religious items that sound spiritual but are not. Organic house church is about Jesus and the Kingdom of God and what it means to be disciples of that Kingdom. Organic house church is about the pursuit of a Jesus-shaped spirituality and a genuine manifestation of the Kingdom of God in your home. Organic house church is God's basic corporate expression of the Kingdom of God. It is a miniature expression of the greater Kingdom, a place where the River of His Spirit flows, where His Presence dwells and where both believers and seekers can touch and taste the *"powers of the age to come"* (Hebrews 6:5) and

# Honey, I Shrunk The Church!

can *"taste and see that the Lord is Good"* (Psalm 34:8).

Ask yourself a question. What do you want people who visit your house church to remember when they leave? Do you want them to leave saying to themselves *"I've tasted and seen God's power and goodness"* or *"Gee, what did you think about his idea that Prince Charles could be the anti-Christ"*? House church is about helping both believers and unbeliever to discover that *"there is a River, the streams whereof make glad the city of God."* Everything else is religious baggage and window dressing.

So, what Christian baggage are you carrying around, and are you willing to leave it at the door as you enter organic house church. If not, your house church experience will probably not be a pleasant one and will probably not last very long, because, as airport officials in Denver discovered, baggage that cannot be handled and properly disposed of will cause the whole operation to eventually shut down.

## O.K., Time To Migrate and Detox

Some of you reading this book *think* you are ready for the shift to organic house church, but in reality you are not. Some of you are still in *"Honey, I shrunk the Church"* mode. You may have flossed, but you haven't detoxed yet. Your values are still those of a religion-shaped spirituality. You still think there should be a pulpit in your living room and a stack of hymnals in the corner, and you should be preaching to the congregation, or at least wowing them with your amazing teaching series on end-time prophecy and the latest candidate for the "anti-Christ."

# Safe Houses of Hope And Prayer

Others of you are still walking around like Jacob Marley in *"A Christmas Carol,"* dragging around your religious baggage and clanging it so loudly that even a dumb post like Ebenezer Scrooge can hear it coming (and you're scaring the locals in the process!). To bend our earlier metaphor to its breaking point, your spiritual dental work not only needs a good flossing, but your entire spiritual body needs a thorough religious detoxing before you can proceed any further (unless you really do want to create another *"Die Heretic"* story in your living room).

Generally speaking, people coming out of the old religion-shaped spirituality, with its set of required values, cannot fully embrace the new values of a Jesus-shaped spirituality and organic house church without first experiencing a profound death-to-self and to the old values which are now passing away.

Several years ago, while on a visit to Spokane, our friend, Wolfgang Simson, gave a talk on *"The 5 Steps of Apostolic Migration."* I was so intrigued and challenged by his talk that I wrote it down and asked my artistically gifted wife to illustrate it. We will use her illustration on the following page to illustrates what follows.

Wolf's thesis was really pretty simple. An Apostolic Migration from old values to new values is sweeping the Church, led by believers in pursuit of a genuine Jesus-Shaped spirituality. But this migration from the old to the new has some specific steps that cannot be short-circuited or avoided.

# Honey, I Shrunk The Church!

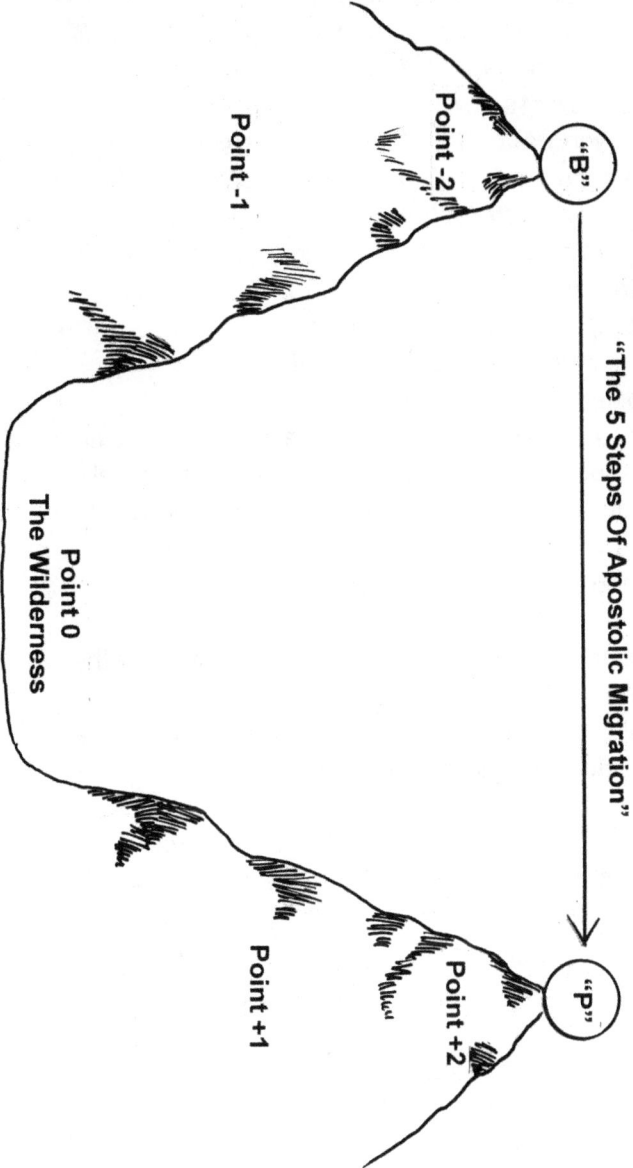

"B"

Point -2

Point -1

Point 0
The Wilderness

Point +1

Point +2

"P"

"The 5 Steps Of Apostolic Migration"

# Safe Houses of Hope And Prayer

The heart of this diagram consists of two mountain peaks. The peak on the left represents what Wolf (following Martin Luther) calls the current *"Babylonian captivity of the Church."* The present day church is being held captive to programs and religious values which no longer serve God's purpose of proclaiming the reality of the

*"An Apostolic Migration from old values to new values is sweeping the Church, led by believers in pursuit of a genuine Jesus-Shaped spirituality."*

Kingdom of God. Church as we know it is preventing Church as God wants it. People are trapped by a religion-shaped spirituality that will not allow them to grow into everything God wants them to be. So, we have labeled this peak *"B"* (for "Babylon").

The mountain peak on the right represents the *"Promised Land"* of organic house church, a Jesus-shaped spirituality that urges believers forward into new manifestations of the Kingdom of God in their homes.

I have labeled this peak *"P."* The line/arrow going from **Peak "B"** directly to **Peak "P"** represents the mistaken belief held by many people that they can quickly migrate directly from the old paradigm to the new paradigm with few (if any) significant changes. Wrong! People holding this view are trying to avoid the personally painful process of dying to themselves and to the old values of their religion-shaped spirituality.

# Honey, I Shrunk The Church!

**Point - 2:** This is where most Christians are today as this new move of God unfolds. Most people at this point are content with where they are in their church experience. When you talk to them about the need to let go of their religion-shaped spirituality and embrace a Jesus-shaped spirituality their response is basically, *"I have no idea what you are talking about."* They are religious square pegs who cannot imagine spiritual round holes.

**Point - 1:** This second point represents people who are no longer satisfied with church as they have known it. These are people who have heard from God about different spiritual values and are beginning to question the religion-shaped spirituality they have been given. They have begun to move in their spirits, but their bodies and their money have not yet moved. They are frustrated square pegs who no longer fit in to their surroundings. Some will move to the next step, while others will not.

**Point  0:** Welcome to the wilderness. This third step represents frustrated square pegs who have finally let go of their religion-shaped spirituality, but they are not yet fully aware that there is a whole new set of spiritual values for them to embrace. This is a critical moment in their journey, when God places religious square pegs on His spiritual lathe and begins the process of spiritual transformation from religious square pegs to spiritual round ones. It is a spiritual reality that it is easier to get a person out of the box than it is to get the box out of the person.  Bad values die hard. For this reason God often engineers a season of wilderness wandering.

## Safe Houses of Hope And Prayer

Following his conversion, the Apostle Paul spent some 11 years in the wilderness of Arabia and Cilicia, dying to self and learning to pursue a Jesus-shaped spirituality, before God sent him on his first missionary journey. It took that long to transform the religious square peg of Saul into the spiritual round peg of Paul. As someone once observed, *"It doesn't take God long to 'make' an Apostle. It takes Him a long time to 'kill' an Apostle."*

*"It is a spiritual reality that it is easier to get a person 'out of the box' than it is to get 'the box' out of the person."*

It is in this spiritual wilderness that we experience a genuine and profound spiritual death to the old values and we undergo a religious detoxification. It is in the wilderness that God begins to round off our sharp religious edges, heal our hurts, wounds, bitterness, anger and other personal baggage left over from our journey out of the old. It is in this spiritual wilderness that God does his greatest work of replacing our religion-shaped spirituality with a Jesus-shaped spirituality.

*"It doesn't take God long to 'make' an Apostle. It takes Him a long time to 'kill' an Apostle."*

Not everyone survives the wilderness experience to emerge healthy at the next Point. A religion-shaped spirituality can be a gnarly little bugger which does not give up easily. Some people are unable to let go of the old values and to fully

# Honey, I Shrunk The Church!

embrace the new ones. Like the Israelites in the wilderness, some people long to return to Egypt, while others perish in the wilderness due to unbelief. But for those who allow God to do his work of religious detoxification and spiritual transformation, they begin to experience a new alignment of their spirits, both with what God is doing and with other people in whom He is doing it. And soon, it's time for them to emerge from the wilderness and to step into the next stage of their journey.

**Point + 1:** This is the stage or point at which people must choose whether or not to leave the past and the wilderness behind and to *"cross over the Jordan"* into the new thing that

> *"The motto of the wilderness is very simple: 'Die well.'"*

God is doing. It is often at this point that attitudes are revealed through statements like, *"You mean I must do house church exclusively?"* O.K., the answer is *"No,"* but the point is *"Why would you WANT to go back?"* This response reveals that the person hasn't fully let go of his religion-shaped spirituality and is still trying to straddle both worlds (the old versus the new). It also means they aren't quite ready to emerge from the wilderness. The motto of the wilderness is very simple: *"Die well."*

**Point + 2:** Welcome to the organic house church movement and that manifestation of it we call *Safe Houses of Hope and Prayer*. At this point you have died to yourself and your journey into a Jesus-shaped spirituality is underway. Your work isn't over. In fact, it's just beginning.

# Safe Houses of Hope And Prayer

## A "Jacob Marley" Evaluation

Take a few minutes to reflect on your own spiritual baggage, including where you are at on your own personal journey into a Jesus-shaped spirituality and organic house church.

**Reflection Question #1 -** Referring back to the *Comparing Values* table on page 47, which set of values reflect where you are currently at in your spiritual experience? Which set of values express where you would like to go?

**Reflection Question #2 -** Where would you place yourself on the *"Apostolic Migration"* diagram on page 52? What is it going to take for you to move on to the next step?

**Reflection Question #3 -** O.K., Jacob Marley, it's time to do a personal inventory of baggage to be thrown overboard. Based on what you have learned in these last three chapters, start doing a personal baggage check in your life. Use the Chart on the following page to help write out your thoughts. As you proceed in this book, you many need to return and add some things to the list, but that's O.K.

# Honey, I Shrunk The Church!

| A "Jacob Marley" Baggage Check | |
|---|---|
| *Values That I Need to Embrace* | *Beliefs, Practices or Attitudes I've Held That Need to Change* |
| | |
| | |
| | |
| | |
| | |
| | |
| | |
| | |
| | |
| | |
| | |
| | |
| | |

# Safe Houses of Hope And Prayer

# Chapter 5

## Life Is Messy (Get Over It)!

The story goes something like this. President Calvin Coolidge returned to the White House after church services one Sunday and was questioned by his wife.

*"What was the preacher's message about?"* she asked.
*"Sin,"* came the reply.
*"Well, what did he have to say,"* asked Mrs. Coolidge. *"He's against it."*

Now that's eloquence in few words.

### The Baggage of Judgmentalism

When it comes to issues of sin, I wish the church could be as simple, as brief and as eloquent as President Coolidge and the preacher. Unfortunately, we often are not.

Let's face reality, shall we. For several years now I have taught a simple maxim in our house church network: *"Life is Messy."* If we look with honest eyes we quickly see that people's lives are a mess. Their families are a mess; their marriages are a mess; their finances are a mess. And that messiness is most often (but not always) caused by sin and its ripple effects. This is true of the non-Christian as well as for the believer. For those of us seeking a Jesus-shaped spirituality in organic house church, our challenge is how to respond to the messiness of life (particularly other people's lives) when it shows up in our living room. Over the years we

# Safe Houses of Hope And Prayer

have had just about everything from divorce to demonic manifestations show up in our living room. That's the challenge (and the blessing) of organic house church. But the messiness of life raises issues of how we deal with issues of sin and its consequences in the lives of those around us as we seek to lead people into the Kingdom of God.

Generally speaking, there are two basic ways such messes can be addressed: 1) We can attempt to create religious rules (*"Do these ten things and God will love you and we may let you back into our house church!"*) designed and intended to clean up messes and prevent sin,  or 2) we can seek God for the inward transformation of the heart and life which overflows in obedience to God.

## Two Causes of House Church Failure

An international leader in the organic house church movement once confided in me that, based on his experience, there are two leading causes of conflict and failure among house churches. My own experience over the years confirms his observation. The two top causes of a failed house church experience are:

*Immature leadership* - This means that the leader (or one of the leaders) of an organic house church is spiritually immature (often resulting from a lack of experience). When a crisis eventually occurs within the house church (as crises usually do), the leader's immaturity causes the  crisis to be poorly handled with the result that the house church is seriously damaged, compromised or even destroyed.

# Life Is Messy!

*Legalism* - Legalism is often a manifestation of a controlling spirit and usually stems from an unbalanced understanding of God and how he works in people's lives. Legalism is a human effort to create in the life of an individual that spiritual change which only the Holy Spirit can create - genuine spiritual transformation. Legalism is the counterfeit of genuine holiness and transformation. It is the response of a religion-shaped spirituality to the messiness of life. For a legalist, pleasing God means creating and adhering to a carefully crafted set of rules which control personal behavior and result in holiness. When a crisis eventually arises a legalist is unable to let go of their tightly-bound religion-shaped spirituality or to resolve it on any terms other than his (or her) set of rules. The result is often wounded people and a splintered church.

> *"Legalism is the counterfeit of genuine holiness and transformation. It is the response of a religion-shaped spirituality to the messiness of life."*

The choice between these two approaches for dealing with issues of sin and the messiness of people's lives, the choice between outward religious conformity to rules versus trusting God for the inward spiritual transformation of the individual, will eventually confront every organic house church. And how you respond will define your ministry and your walk.

I want to urge you to believe God for the inward spiritual transformation of people's hearts, in spite of the messiness of their lives, rather than allowing yourself to walk in a spirit of control and religious legalism. Every ministry, including the

# Safe Houses of Hope And Prayer

organic house church which meets in your house, will eventually be defined by two things: What it stands against, and what it stands for. As organic house churches and *Safe Houses of Hope And Prayer*, we must stand against sin and the

> *". . . you (can't) fight spiritual darkness with man-made religious rules."*

kingdom of darkness in all of its manifestations, and against any spirit of control and outward religious conformity which believes and teaches that you can fight spiritual darkness with man-made religious rules. We stand for the Kingdom of God in all of its righteousness and holiness, and for the genuine spiritual transformation of the individual heart which will overflow in obedience to God.

## The Promise of Inward Spiritual Transformation

*"Behold, the days are coming, declares the LORD, when I will make a new covenant with the house of Israel and the house of Judah, not like the covenant that I made with their fathers on the day when I took them by the hand to bring them out of the land of Egypt, my covenant that they broke, though I was their husband, declares the LORD. For this is the covenant that I will make with the house of Israel after those days, declares the LORD: I will put my law within them, and I will write it on their hearts. And I will be their God, and they shall be my people. And no longer shall each one teach his neighbor and each his brother, saying, 'Know the LORD,' for they shall all know me, from the least of them to the greatest, declares the LORD. For I will forgive their iniquity, and I will remember their sin no more."* (Jeremiah 31:31-34)

# Life Is Messy!

This passage from the Old Testament book of Jeremiah represents one of the greatest and most important Old Testament promises regarding the people of God, the Law of God and true spirituality. Under the Old Testament covenant true spirituality was defined primarily by outward personal conformity to the 612 commandments of the Law (no, not just the 10 Commandments). The history of ancient Israel was the story of the consistent failure and inability of the Israelites to keep the 612 commandments of the Law. This failure culminated in the ministry of the Prophet Jeremiah, the prophet of the covenant, who prophesied the destruction and captivity of God's people for their continued unfaithfulness to the Covenant and its 612 requirements.

Yet, in the midst of this 52-chapter-long condemnation of the people for their spiritual adultery Jeremiah offers this stunning promise: A day is coming when God will replace the Old Covenant of outward conformity with a NEW COVENANT of inward transformation: *"I will put my law within them, and I will write it on their hearts. And I will be their God, and they shall be my people."* God, through Jeremiah, was promising a coming day when outward religious conformity to a set of external rules (either God's or man's) would be replaced with the true spirituality of a transformed life whose highest desire will be to obey God

> *"The history of ancient Israel was the story of the consistent failure and inability of the Israelites to keep the 612 commandments of the Law."*

because His Law will be written on their hearts.

# Safe Houses of Hope And Prayer

## Jesus and Spiritual Transformation

The New Testament is the record of the unfolding of that New Covenant. Jesus highlighted this difference between outward religious conformity and inward spiritual transformation in His encounter with the rich young ruler in Luke

> *". . . a spiritually transformed person will want to obey all of Jesus' commandments for love's sake, if for no other reason."*

18:18-23. This man had led a life dedicated to outward religious conformity to the requirements of the Law. *"All these things I have kept from my youth,"* he declared in response to Jesus. Perfect conformity to all the rules. But Jesus saw things differently. Jesus saw a heart bound by religious legalism and self-righteousness, and in desperate need of spiritual transformation. So, to highlight that need, Jesus asked him to do the one thing an untransformed heart could not do, *"One thing you still lack, sell all that you possess, and distribute it to the poor, and you shall have treasure in heaven; and come, follow me."* There was nothing in the Law which required such an action. But the New Covenant isn't about the requirements of the Law. The New Covenant is about the condition of the heart. Jesus exposed a condition which the Law couldn't address.

And this highlights the conflict between outward religious conformity to rules (including the 612 commandments of the Law) and inward spiritual transformation. A religious person can keep all of the Law yet never experience true spirituality, or a genuine spiritual transformation. But a spiritually transformed person will want to obey all of Jesus' commandments for love's sake, if for no other reason.

## St. Paul & Spiritual Transformation

The Apostle Paul understood the difference between the Old Covenant of outward religious conformity and the New Covenant of inward spiritual transformation, and he explained it to the Church in Corinth in 2 Corinthians Chapter 3. Paul understood the promise of Jeremiah Chapter 31 and in 2 Corinthians 3 he claimed that it was now being fulfilled in the ministry of the Holy Spirit in the lives of believers:

*"You yourselves are our letter of recommendation, written on our hearts, to be known and read by all. And you show that you are a letter from Christ delivered by us, written not with ink but with the Spirit of the living God, not on tablets of stone but on tablets of human hearts."* (2 Corinthians 3:2-3)

Paul goes on to contrast the Old Covenant of outward conformity to the Law and its 612 requirements with the New Covenant and its promise of inward spiritual transformation. According to Paul, the Old Covenant was a ministry of death which offered only a fading glory, whereas the New Covenant represents a ministry of the Spirit which offers a greater glory. The Old Covenant was a ministry of the letter which killed, whereas the New Covenant was a ministry of the Spirit which gives life. The Old Covenant was a ministry of condemnation (i.e., because the Law condemns us for our unrighteousness) whereas the New Covenant is a ministry of righteousness that gives us the very righteousness - the righteousness of Christ - which the Old Covenant demanded but could not provide. The Old Covenant represented a fading glory whereas the New Covenant represents a glory which abides and abounds. Paul's punch line comes in 2 Corinthians 3:17-18:

*"Now the Lord is the Spirit, and where the Spirit of the Lord is, there is freedom. And we all, with unveiled face, beholding the glory of the Lord, are being transformed into the same image from one degree of glory to another. For this comes from the Lord who is the Spirit."*

The Spirit of God brings both transformation and liberty. It sets people free from the impossible demands of outward religious conformity and religious legalism. And the Spirit of God under this new and glorious covenant brings

*"The Spirit of God brings both transformation and liberty."*

about something the Law never could - inward spiritual transformation which results in our being transformed into the very image of God in Christ!

## Legalism Vs. Transformation

O.K., how does this apply to *Safe Houses of Hope And Prayer* and the organic house church which meets in your house. Let me begin by saying that, when it comes to sin, *Safe Houses of Hope And Prayer* agrees with President Coolidge and his pastor: *We're against it!*

Here is where life gets complicated and messy. You see, in

# Life Is Messy!

order to deal with or prevent the sins which they see in others, people and ministries are constantly tempted to create rules of outward religious conformity. We fail to comprehend Paul's description of the Law in 2 Corinthians 3 as representing a ministry of death and which offers only a fleeting, temporary glory. All too often we fail to realize that, if the Law of God brought only death and condemnation, any laws and rules of men can only do worse! Religious legalism is like fools gold. In the end it is a worthless disappointment, but one which leads many people astray before the truth is discovered.

But because men are sometimes desperate for any kind of glory, however fleeting, they will pursue even a temporary and fading glory which they can control, rather than a greater abounding glory which only God by His Spirit can give. And there's the rub. A religion-shaped spirituality made up of legalism and outward religious conformity places trust in ourselves to conquer sin and to clean up life's messes by our own efforts. But a Jesus-shaped spirituality seeking spiritual transformation must always trust God, for He alone gives His Spirit without measure.

> *"All too often we fail to realize that, if the Law of God brought only death and condemnation, any laws and rules of men can only do worse!"*

This is why Paul could write to the Corinthians and say, *"And such confidence we have through Christ toward God."* Paul's confidence was not in his ability to control the Corinthians into godly behavior with religious rules, or even in the ability of the Corinthians themselves to live by some set of outward religious rules. Paul's confidence was in the surpassing power and ability of God to transform the Corinthians and to write His Law on their hearts.

## Can You Illustrate This?

I can, but it requires a story. Let me begin this story by saying that I have the personal blessing of having been married to the same wonderful woman for some 36 years. Neither I nor my wife have ever had sex with anyone else. It is a joy we

> *"Paul's confidence was in the surpassing power and ability of God to transform the Corinthians and to write His Law on their hearts."*

have shared only with each other. We believe in biblical sexual purity. We have lived and have sought to model sexual purity both in our personal lives and in our ministry.

But a few years ago, as we were partnering in an outreach, the leadership team of which I was a part was challenged by someone in the ministry who demanded that we agree with them that two unmarried adults of the opposite sex sleeping in the same room (but not in the same bed) constituted the sin of adultery. We disagreed. While such behavior might not be wise, there are many unwise behaviors in life which are not in and of themselves sin. But to consistently apply such an interpretation of Scripture to other situations would mean that two men sleeping in the same room constituted homosexuality; that two women sleeping in the same room constituted lesbianism; a person and an animal sleeping in the same room would constitute bestiality . . . well, you get the point. They went on to say that unless we accepted their interpretation of adultery we were twisting Scripture and tolerating adultery, and they could no longer support or be involved with our ministry. Yep, it turned ugly.

While their interpretation on its surface might appeal to some as spiritual, it is nothing less than fool's gold, outward religious legalism masquerading as spirituality. While it might be well intended, it was none-the-less a ministry of death and condemnation to all who might embrace it (not to mention a misinterpretation and misapplication of God's Word).[14]

What does this mean for *Safe Houses of Hope And Prayer* and organic house church? And why is this an issue? It means that in both word and deed our message MUST be that we are not here to call anyone to obey our set of rules. We are here to proclaim the Kingdom of God and liberty to the captives. We are here to proclaim that God wants to transform people from the inside out, to deliver them from the ministry of death and condemnation and to introduce them to the abiding and abounding glory of God in the face of Christ. To the extent that we impose our man-made rules of outward religious conformity, we short-circuit the work of God's Spirit and offer the fool's gold of believing that personal transformation will come as the result of keeping a set of rules.

---

[14]As is often the case, there was more to this story. The couple in question had been living together for 10 years, but their recent journey into faith had caused them to re-assess their relationship. I had the privilege of officiating their wedding a few months later.

# Safe Houses of Hope And Prayer

## Be Defined By What You Are For!
*(Not by what you are against!)*

As I said earlier, when it comes to sin, we are against it. We are also against the fool's gold and fading glory of outward religious conformity to rules which appear spiritual, but which are nothing short of r e l i g i o u s   l e g a l i s m masquerading as spirituality.

> *"No person, ministry or church can allow themselves to be defined solely by the things they are against."*

No person, ministry or church can allow themselves to be defined solely by the things they are against. It is important that you and all those to whom you minister in the hope of leading them into the Kingdom of God, know what you stand FOR. Organic house church and *Safe Houses of Hope and Prayer* stands for the following things which, in my opinion, are God's antidote to religious legalism and outward religious conformity:

***1. We stand FOR God's Unconditional Love.*** People in our Postmodern culture today have known many things over the years: sex, drugs, violence, and even religious people. But most of them have never known or experienced unconditional love from either God or His people.  We want to change that.  The importance of offering God's unconditional love to people cannot be overstated. Writing for *Focus on the Family*, Christian author Ken Gire summed it up well:

# Life Is Messy!

*"When asked what the secret of living the Christian life was, Augustine replied: 'Love God, and do as you please.' The thought of that is both liberating and confining. Liberating because it means we are free to do whatever we want. Confining because it means our love for God sets the boundaries of that freedom. It guides every thought, every action, every conversation. And it does so every minute of the day, every day of our life. Instead of a Byzantine complexity of laws to regulate every detail of our life, we have only one. The love of God. When that is at the heart of who we are, it changes what we do. And it changes something else. How we will be judged. St. John of the Cross once said that 'at the evening of our day we shall be judged by our loving.' As we look back over our day, what we have done is not as important as how we have done it. Better to do little with much love than much with little love. For without love, whatever we do will be dismissed with a judicial wave of heaven's hand as just so many trivial pursuits (1 Corinthians 13:1-3)."*

We believe that God, by His Holy Spirit, is the *"Hound of Heaven"* who pursues each of us through our many vain wanderings with a love that never sleeps, that never grows faint, that never retreats, and that never presents us with a list of rules which says: *"Do these 10 things and I will love you."*

**2. We stand FOR God's Grace, His Unmerited Favor.** Grace is God's unmerited love and favor. And we can no more earn God's favor after we believe than we could earn it before we believed. At some level, those who walk in a spirit of control, religious legalism and outward religious conformity to rules believe that God's love and favor can somehow be earned, or at least maintained, by what they do. And they expect others to believe and do the same. They have a genuinely hard time believing that God loves people for who they are, warts and all. But that is the nature of Grace.

**3. We stand FOR the Spiritual Transformation of each individual person by the Holy Spirit.** We share Paul's confidence in God's ability to transform every individual and to write His law upon their hearts with the result that they will love Him and obey all His commandments as the outflow of a transformed heart. That is what Scripture teaches, that is what Jesus did, and that is what we believe. And until that day of personal spiritual transformation arrives, our calling is to demonstrate to them God's unconditional love and to offer them God's unmerited favor.

**4. Finally, we believe in and stand FOR a soon coming day of God's gracious visitation in power, in blessing and in spiritual transformation.** We believe that the River of God's Spirit, the River of Ezekiel 47, is preparing to flow in great power to cleanse, to heal, to draw people to Himself and to spiritually transform us, our homes and the organic church which meets in our houses. In the day of His power and visitation God will do more in a day to deal with our sin and the messiness of our lives than all the religious rules of men could accomplish in a lifetime. But God is looking for vessels and channels through which the River of His power and blessing can flow unimpeded by human control, by religious legalism or by any man-made religious rule.

# Life Is Messy!

## More Work On Your "Jacob Marley" List

***Reflection Question #1*** - Discuss this statement: *"I am a 'fix-it' person who is constantly trying to 'fix' people. I believe that the messiness of other people's lives would be solved if they would just live their lives by the same rules I live by."* So, how's that working for you?

***Reflection Question #2*** - Based on your own understanding and what you have read in this chapter, what is the difference between the personal holiness of outward conformity and legalism, and the personal holiness of inward transformation by the Holy Spirit.

***Reflection Question #3*** - Reflect on the following statement from earlier in the Chapter:

*"Grace is God's unmerited love and favor. And we can no more earn God's favor after we believe than we could earn it before we believed."*

What is the difference between legalism and obedience out of love for God?

***Reflection Question #4*** - What legalistic behaviors do you see in yourself that you might need to add to your ***"Jacob Marley" Baggage List,*** which we have conveniently reproduced on the following page?

# Safe Houses of Hope And Prayer

| A "Jacob Marley" Baggage Check | |
|---|---|
| Values That I Need to Embrace | Beliefs, Practices or Attitudes I've Held That Need to Change |
| | |
| | |
| | |
| | |
| | |
| | |
| | |
| | |
| | |
| | |
| | |
| | |
| | |

# Chapter 6

## Four Organic Church Priorities

*"And they were continually devoting themselves to the apostles' teaching and to fellowship, to the breaking of bread and to prayer."* (Acts 2:42, NASB)

The New Testament book of Acts is the record of a 32-year-long spiritual outpouring and awakening that began on the Day of Pentecost and lasted through the end of the book. As the organic house church movement prepares for another spiritual outpouring and awakening in our own day, I believe there are some things we can learn from those early believers and their response to that move of God's Spirit in their day.

So, take a moment, find your Bible and read this passage: Acts 2:41-47. Done? O.K., this passage occurs early in the post-Pentecost life of the early church (we're talking a matter of days). It gives us a snap shot in time of what the normal life in the early house churches of the New Testament was like in the wake of that spiritual outpouring. It helps us answer the question, *"What did they do on a regular basis?"* Whatever those things were, we should probably give special attention to them in our organic house churches, too. So, we're going to focus our attention on the four things which are mentioned in Acts 2:42. We'll call these *"Four Organic Church Priorities."*

Now, how do we know that these four items were priorities

for the New Testament Church? Because the Scriptures tell us that those early believers were *"continually devoting themselves"* to these four things. The word translated *"continually devoting"* (Greek: <u>proskartereo</u>) means *"to be continually steadfast"* or *"to be devoted"* to something. The same word phrase is found in Acts 1:14 where the disciples in the Upper Room were described as *"continually devoting themselves to prayer"* (See also Acts 6:4). The adverb form of this Greek word is commonly translated *"perseverance."* The idea here is simple. Those early believers persevered at four specific things - priorities - which demand our perseverance, too.

***Organic Church Priority # 1: Teaching.*** Because the issue of "teaching" is a recurring element in the life of the Church, we will have more to say about it in this book as we move forward (specifically, see Chapter 13 and 14). But we can start that conversation here.

The Greek word for *"teaching"* Acts 2:42 (<u>didache</u>) suggests some kind of formal instruction regarding a body of information. In other words, the house churches of the New Testament demonstrated a conscious commitment to formal instruction in the things of God. This verse specifically refers to *"the Apostles' teaching"* or doctrine. That Apostolic teaching has been preserved for us in the Scriptures of the New Testament. The

*"The early New Testament house churches considered teaching a priority, something which required perseverance and commitment."*

regular public reading and teaching of the Scriptures should be a part of the ordinary life of the house church. And Ephesians 4:11-12 tells us that God has given gifted Teachers to the Church for the purpose of expounding the Scriptures and *"equipping . . . the saints for the work of service"* (We will have more to say about the role of Teachers in Chapter 8). The early New Testament house churches considered teaching a priority, something which required perseverance and commitment.

But we need to make two important observations. *First*, teaching in the early church was NOT to the exclusion of everything else. Teaching in the house church was important, as opposed to optional, but it was not exclusive or dominant either.

*Second*, the goal of biblical teaching is **NOT** knowledge, but a transformed life. *"Knowledge makes arrogant,"* Paul warned the house churches of Corinth, *"but love edifies"* (builds up). An over-taught church will be smart, but powerless. In the Kingdom of God, knowledge is NOT power. Just because you know all of the Greek words for healing doesn't mean you will be able to heal anyone.

We need to pursue and persevere in teaching the truths of God in a way that transforms our lives (and those of our hearers) into the image of Christ, and causes us to love God with all our heart, soul, mind and strength, and our

*"An over-taught church will be smart, but powerless. In the Kingdom of God, knowledge is NOT power."*

neighbors as ourselves. After all, these are the two greatest commandments. We will have more to say about the role and importance of teaching in house church in Chapter 13.

***Organic Church Priority # 2:  Fellowship.*** I would dare to say that most Christians in traditional institutional churches never achieve or experience genuine fellowship (what I would prefer to call genuine community). Why? Because genuine fellowship is messy, takes work and requires perseverance. For time pressed leaders, it is much

> *"We share a common life in the Kingdom of God and drink from a common River of His Spirit in the bond of Christ."*

easier to teach people to death with impressive Bible notes in PowerPoint presentations than it is to work through the personal issues which stand in the way of genuine community. And lectures you can control are easier than dialogues which you can't.

Our English word translated *"fellowship"* is the Greek word *koinonia* which comes from the Greek word *koine*, meaning *"common."* Fellowship is the holding of certain things in common. In the life of the organic house church it is a mutual sharing of our lives together. We share a common life in the Kingdom of God and drink from a common River of His Spirit in the bond of Christ.

The desire for genuine *koinonia* was not new in the ancient world, nor was it exclusively Christian. The Classical Greek

# Four Organic Church Priorities

philosophers had envisioned a utopian fellowship that they described as *koinonia*. But all classical attempts to achieve this *koinonia* by human effort had failed miserably. But now, through the death and resurrection of Christ and the outpouring of the Holy Spirit, God had accomplished in the Church and the Kingdom of God what the efforts of men throughout the ages had never achieved: *genuine fellowship*. And this fellowship, this genuine *koinonia*, was manifested in the organic house churches of the New Testament where believers shared their lives with one another. They shared meals together in one another's homes. They prayed together, endured persecution together, worshiped together and, at times, they even died together. They preferred one another's company above all others and gave sacrificially to meet each other's needs. To express it in contemporary terms for today, these early house churches were made up of people who loved to hang out together. They shared an affinity - an attraction based on common interests - that surpassed the natural - it was supernatural. True *koinonia* or fellowship means that as Christians we share a common life in the Kingdom of God.

A quick word is in order at this point about genuine *koinonia* or community versus pseudo-community. In genuine community the reality is that baggage happens and this frequently results in conflicts. But mature believers look past the conflict and work together to *"bear one another's burdens"* (Galatians 6:2) and help each other unpack their baggage and resolve their conflicts. Unfortunately, this is a new experience for many people who have only experienced the pseudo-community of most churches (traditional and otherwise).

# Safe Houses of Hope And Prayer

In his excellent book *The Different Drum* Dr. M. Scott Peck describes pseudo-community this way:

*"The essential dynamic of pseudo-community is conflict avoidance. The absence of conflict in a group is not by itself diagnostic. Genuine community may experience lovely and sometimes lengthy periods free from conflict. But that is because they have learned how to dal with conflict rather than avoid it. Pseudo-community is conflict-avoiding; true community is conflict resolving."* [15]

Genuine community, genuine *koinonia* requires intimacy, vulnerability and conflict resolution with both God and men. Genuine *koinonia* requires a willingness to work through differences, baggage and conflict. If we are to be

> *"Genuine koinonia requires a willingness to work through differences, baggage and conflict."*

successful as organic house churches and as *Safe Houses of Hope and Prayer*, then we must pursue genuine community in our house churches and create a safe place where it can take place.

***Organic Church Priority # 3:    The breaking of bread.*** Have you ever sung the old spiritual *"Let Us Break Bread Together On Our Knees"*? Have you ever wondered what it meant?   What is *"the breaking of bread"*? This particular Greek phrase only appears twice in the New Testament. In

---

[15]M. Scott Peck, ***The Different Drum: Community Making and Peace,*** 2nd Edition (New York: Touchstone/Simon & Schuster, 1998) p. 88

# Four Organic Church Priorities

addition to our present passage in Acts 2, the other occurrence is in Luke 24:35, *"And they began to relate their experiences on the road and how He was recognized by them in the breaking of the bread."*

This passage from Luke records the appearance of Christ to the disciples on the road to Emmaus. The risen Christ agreed to stay and dine with the disciples who had not yet recognized who He really was. Then,

*"it came about that when He had reclined at the table with them, He took the bread and blessed it, and breaking it, He began giving it to them. And their eyes were opened and they recognized Him; and He vanished from their sight."*

In what was essentially a re-enactment of their final meal together, the disciples recognized Jesus in *"the breaking of the bread."*

It should come as no surprise to us that those early New Testament believers were fond of sharing meals together. And following the pattern of Jesus on the night of His betrayal, at some point during the meal, they would observe *"the breaking of the bread"* in a manner that commemorated that final meal of Jesus with His disciples.

Today, we call it *"observing the Lord's Supper."* For far too long institutional Christianity has separated *"the breaking of bread"* from the ordinary life of the body of believers. We have worked to surround it with a mystique by requiring the supervision of a uniquely ordained person to supervise the event and even to administer special words of institution in order to give the sacrament some magical validity.

## Safe Houses of Hope And Prayer

But no where in the New Testament do we see such a ritualized observance of the Lord's Supper. Quite the contrary. The simplicity, importance and centrality of observing the Lord's Supper in the New Testament Church can be seen in Paul's words to the Church in Corinth:

*"For I received from the Lord what I also delivered to you, that the Lord Jesus on the night when he was betrayed took bread, and when he had given thanks, he broke it, and said, 'This is my body which is for you. Do this in remembrance of me.' In the same way also he took the cup, after supper, saying, 'This cup is the new covenant in my blood. Do this, as often as you drink it, in remembrance of me.' For as often as you eat this bread and drink the cup, you proclaim the Lord's death until he comes."*(1 Corinthians 11:23-26)

The good news is that the organic house church movement is rediscovering the importance of sharing meals together on a regular basis, during which we remember and celebrate *"the breaking of the bread,"* the Lord's Supper.

Do not take this point too lightly. When we in our organic house churches break bread together and observe the Lord's Supper, we are standing as *"the Church Militant"* in spiritual and mystical union with *"the*

*". . . the Angelic host gaze at us in wonder, longing to understand spiritual truths we take for granted."*

*Church Triumphant,"* together in spiritual and mystical union with Christ our Head. And that is a spiritual truth and a mystery so profound that the Angelic host gaze at us in wonder, longing to understand spiritual truths we take for granted.

***Organic Church Priority # 4: Prayer.*** Let's establish some context here. The Church had just spent ten days with 120 people locked away in an upper room fasting and praying together for the promised *"power from on high"* (and their prayers had been answered!). That's a pretty good indication that the early church placed a high priority on fasting and prayer (fasting and prayer shows up again in the life of the Church in Acts 13 in the Church of Antioch - resulting in Paul's first missionary journey).

Not too long ago I had a conversation with an individual who was attending a local megachurch which averaged a weekly attendance of around 6,000. He told me how he had attended a recent prayer meeting and was saddened to discover that from a church of 6,000 people, only about 40 people showed up for prayer. Not exactly what I would call *"persevering in prayer."* Now, while you and I may groan at that situation, when it comes to persevering in specific intentional prayer, are we really much better?

> *"Prayer is the life-breath of the soul and of the Church."*

Prayer is the life-breath of the soul and of the Church. Oswald Chambers once observed, *"Prayer does not prepare us for the greater work. Prayer IS the greater work."* It will be during times of prayer and worship, both personally and as a worshiping Church that the Holy Spirit will speak with encouragement and guidance (see Acts 13:1), and that spiritual gifts will begin to manifest and function.

# Safe Houses of Hope And Prayer

Perseverance means we work at learning how to pray and minister together. Several years ago I was conducting a home fellowship leader's meeting for a Church and I was emphasizing the importance of open prayer together. One of the leaders (a physician) spoke up, *"You know,"* he said with a wry grin, *"praying together is sort of like skinny-dipping together; it takes some getting use to."* Yep. Absent the skinny-dipping, we call that perseverance.

The organic house churches of the New Testament were committed to prayer, and God heard and answered their prayers in powerful ways, *"And when they had prayed, the place where they had gathered together was shaken, and they were all filled with the Holy Spirit, and began to speak the word of God with boldness."*

> *"Perseverance means we work at learning how to pray and minister together."*

## Living Out Your Priorities

Do you know the difference between a religious rule and a spiritual priority. The answer is flexibility. It is a short journey from a spiritual priority to a religious rule and finally to a legalistic requirement. A religious rule says we must have a weekly teaching or we aren't really doing church. Flexibility says that there will be times of good and powerful teaching, brought by one person or by several, but there will also be times of no teaching because we are feeling called to focus on worship and prayer instead, or we are sensing a need for a lot personal ministry to the needs of the body. Flexibility

# Four Organic Church Priorities

means we understand biblical priorities, but we are also sensitive to the needs of the body and to the leading of the Holy Spirit whenever we meet.

*Reflection Question #1* - What did you learn from this chapter about organic house church priorities that you did not know before?

*Reflection Question #2* - Which of these four priorities is over-emphasized in your house church? Which one is under-emphasized. What can you do to start changing this situation?

# Safe Houses of Hope And Prayer

# Chapter 7

## Who's In Charge Here, Anyway?

Let's you and I take a quick trip back in time to the 1$^{st}$ Century A.D. If you and I could visit a 1$^{st}$ Century New Testament Church, we might notice several things. For example, we might immediately notice that it met in someone's home. We might also notice the absence of any Bibles. The New Testament was still being written. Copies of the Gospels and Paul's various letters might be circulating and read aloud during the meeting, but most of the Scripture readings would be from the Old Testament. The "potluck" would be pretty simple food: bread, oil, wine, fruit, vegetables and maybe some fish or other meat.

You and I would be surrounded by ordinary people: fishermen, leather workers, potters, bakers, slaves, freed-men (former slaves), Jews and non-Jews (Gentiles). The house would be teeming with men, women and children.

> *"The meeting would be led by people like yourself. Maybe people you already knew, people like your next door neighbors."*

And then there was the leadership. The meeting would be led by people like yourself. Maybe people you already knew, people like your next door neighbors. And this would probably raise some questions for you, like, *"How could these ordinary people lead a church?"* Good question, and it deserves an answer.

# Safe Houses of Hope And Prayer

When you and I read the New Testament Book of Acts (the story of the growth and spread of the early Church) we discover that many New Testament Churches got started and initially functioned without designated or appointed leaders (called elders). That step came later as the Churches grew and matured. And even when leaders were appointed (see Acts 14:23) we discover that all of those leaders were converts from either paganism or Judaism with little or no training or experience in what it takes to lead a church. For example, in the New Testament both Timothy and Titus led house churches (perhaps even groups of house churches).

> *". . . these were ordinary people who learned by watching and doing, and they corrected their 'mistakes' along the way."*

What were their qualifications? They traveled and hung out with the Apostle Paul and watched what he did in the various house churches during his travels. And apart from receiving an occasional letter from Paul with notes of encouragement and a few bits of advice, that was it!

I could tell similar stories about other New Testament leaders like Apollos or Aquila and Priscilla. But the short lesson here is that these were ordinary people who learned by watching and doing, and they corrected their mistakes along the way (on the job training, you might say!). There were no books on pastoral care and biblical leadership. There were no Bible college or seminary graduates, no ordained or credentialed clergy, no professional staff. But God called out and raised up leaders, giving them on the job training among fellow believers who probably had far less Biblical knowledge and experience than you or I have today.

If God could use them, He can use you! If they could do it, so can you! As we observed in our previous book in this series, Jesus of Nazareth entrusted His Church to twelve non-professional, uneducated fishermen and social outcasts. Not exactly top graduates from the leadership academy, by today's standards. How effective was their leadership? They turned the Roman Empire upside down for the Kingdom of God. Two thousand years later, our top graduates and highly educated professional staff are still working on reaching New Jersey.

## Leaders Who K.I.S.S.

You're probably familiar with K.I.S.S. No, I'm not referring to the rock band with Gene Simmons and the boys (at least I think they're all boys - word on the street is that they are really demons in disguise!). I'm referring to the acronym which stands for *"Keep It Simple Stupid."* This is an acronym and a motto

*". . . the more complex you make the practice of organic house church, the more important you make yourself look, but the less important you actually become."*

which should be memorized and practiced by every house church leader. Organic house church is frequently referred to as simple church. Why? Because it really IS simple (Duh?!). And therein lies the potential danger and pitfall for organic house church leaders - keeping things simple.

## Safe Houses of Hope And Prayer

As the leader (or elder) of the organic church which meets in your house, the more complex you make the practice of organic house church, the more important you make yourself look, but the less important you actually

> *"One of the first and primary callings of any leader is to reproduce and multiply himself (or herself) in as many lives as possible."*

become. Leaders who promote a complicated model of organic house church are sending a not-so-subtle message which says, *"You have to know everything I know before you can do what I do."*

By offering a complicated model of house church, centered around themselves, leaders make themselves look important, but in reality they are diminishing their true importance by reducing their effectiveness for the Kingdom of God. Your complicated self-centered model will reach fewer people and make fewer disciples because very few people can do what you do. One of the first and primary callings of any leader is to reproduce and multiply himself (or herself) in as many lives as possible (2 Timothy 2:2). The more complicated you make that leadership multiplication process, the greater the likelihood of failure, and the less effective for the Kingdom you will become. Decide now which you want. Do you want to be **important** in the eyes of men? Or do you want to be **effective** for the Kingdom of God.

As leaders we must always measure our activities by two things: Objective and relevance. Ask yourself these two questions. **First,** *"What is my objective?"* Is your objective to

## Who's In Charge Here, Anyway?

fill your house with people who come for your awesome bible teaching and who hang on your every word? Or is your objective to build a biblical community of healthy believers who are being equipped to leave

> *"As leaders we must always measure our activities by two things: objective and relevance."*

your house, to reproduce what they have seen, experienced and learned and to plant an organic house church in their home to reach their friends and neighbors with the Kingdom of God? The **second** question is this: *"Is what I am doing actually relevant to achieving my objective?"* As Robert Coleman once observed,

*"Objective and relevance - these are the crucial issues of our work. Both are interrelated, and the measure by which they are made compatible will largely determine the significance of all our activity. Merely because we are busy, or even skilled, doing something does not necessarily mean that we are getting anything accomplished. The question must always be asked. Is it worth doing? And does it get the job done?"* [16]

You may be the greatest Bible teacher since the Apostle Paul (probably not, but I'm willing to pretend for a moment). But if your house church becomes a complicated and non-reproducible model centered around you and your amazing ability to teach, your effectiveness for the Kingdom of God

---

[16]Robert Coleman *The Master Plan of Evangelism* (Tarrytown, New York: Fleming H. Revell Company, 1972), page 11.

will quickly diminish for the simple reason that the average person in your house church cannot reproduce and multiply what you do in their own house (selling CDs and posting yourself on YouTube don't count). You have unwittingly turned those around you into a herd of spiritual mules who will never be able to reproduce. They and your house church are now just one generation away from extinction, and they have you to thank. Happy?

## So, Who IS In Charge Here?

By now you should have noticed that I have tactfully avoided answering this original question . . . until now. Not being able to put it off any longer, here's the answer: **You are!** O.K., the

> *"Jesus Himself wants to visit and lead the Church which gathers and meets in your house."*

answer is really two fold. **First,** YOU are in charge. You are the one called by God to lead the simple, organic house church (the *Safe House of Hope And Prayer*) which meets in your house! **Second**, Jesus is in charge! And by means of the indwelling Holy Spirit, Jesus Himself wants to visit and lead the Church which gathers and meets in your house. Make sure you take the time as a group to seek Him and to ask Him what it is He wants to do in, among and through you!

On a human level we always want to know who is leading the meeting. And Scripture does give us some answers to this question. I believe that Scripture actually describes seven (7) leadership callings. These are NOT offices but job descriptions which describe how people are to function in the church body. Every house church, because it is an extended family, has a father and/or mother figure of experience and wisdom who leads it. We call these individuals elders and deacons. These individuals are the core of New Testament leadership.

In addition to elders and deacons, Scripture also talks about God-appointed itinerant workers who serve and minister among a network, a city or a region. They make up what is commonly referred to as the 5-fold ministry of apostles, prophets,

*"These seven callings are intended by God to function as a leadership team, each with a unique role, to oversee and encourage the health and growth of the body."*

evangelists, pastors and teachers. These are the 5-fold ministry gifts. In Acts 15 the Apostles and elders came together to form an Apostolic Council to solve problems, make decisions and set policy. These seven callings are intended by God to function as a leadership team, each with a unique role, to oversee and encourage the health and growth of the body. Over time, as your house church matures and grows, God will call out and raise up people to function in all of these areas. For now, I only want to treat the two primary leadership callings of the individual house church. We will deal more in-depth with the 5-Fold leadership gifts in the next Chapter.

*Elders -* Every extended family has a father or mother figure who leads the extended family. The same should be true of the house church family. Generally speaking, elders (as the

# Safe Houses of Hope And Prayer

Greek term *presbuteros* suggests) are people of age, wisdom and maturity who know and understand the needs of their particular house church families. (See 1 Timothy 3:1-7 and 1 Peter 5:1-4).

The biblical responsibility of an elder is essentially two-fold, summed up by two Greek words. **First,** Elders function as big picture people (Greek: *episkopos*) referred to as overseers. In this function elders oversee the life, the functioning and the administration of the house church. They keep their eye on the overall needs of the church body.

> *"Elders are to be mentors, not dictators."*

**Second,** elders are also shepherds (Greek: *poimen*). In this role Elders are responsible is to feed and tend the flock. Is someone in their house church hurting spiritually, struggling financially, sick, stumbling into drugs or alcohol? The calling of the Elder is to reach out to them like a parent would to a hurting child. (BTW - A house church shepherd tends his own house church flock. A 5-fold shepherd tends several house churches).

**Finally,** elders are **not** given authority to lord it over those they serve. Indeed, they are prohibited from it (see 1 Peter 5:3). Elders are to be mentors, not dictators. Elders lead by their personal example of Christ-likeness toward those they serve. They also work with the Apostles to solve problems and set policy for the house churches (See Acts 15).

**Deacons -** These are the people of service and compassion who function as the need assessors of the body. The calling of deacons first appears on the radar screen of the early church in Acts 6:1-6. They were to be spirit-filled individuals of wisdom and good reputation. Their function in the organic life of the Church is to identify and know the practical needs of the house church and to communicate those needs

> *"(Deacons) are the people of service and compassion who function as the need assessors of the body."*

to the rest of the leadership. Deacons are the uniquely and powerfully gifted servants of the body who work closely with the Apostles and elders to see that the compassionate and physical needs of the body are met (Acts 6:1-4).

### Is Leadership A "Boys Only Club"?

We saw this issue of women in leadership earlier in Chapter 2 with Susanna Wesley, and again in the ministry of John Wesley, who placed women in leadership roles within his Class structure. Funny how the old becomes new again . . . and again.

> *"The New Testament pattern clearly suggests that it was primarily men who served as elders, while both men and women served as deacons."*

The New Testament pattern clearly suggests that it was *primarily* men who served as elders, while both men and women served as deacons. But this pattern was ***not*** absolute

97

or exclusive (re-read that last part, please). Paul acknowledged Aquila and Priscilla as his co-workers or fellow-laborers in the Lord (see Romans 16:3). We also know that Phoebe served a deaconess in the Church in Rome (Romans 16:1), and it is clear from 1 Timothy 3 that the qualifications for both elders and deacons are virtually identical. That includes the requirement that both be the husband of one wife, suggesting that the issue is not gender but marital fidelity.

Then, in Romans 16:7 Paul says, *"Greet Andronicus and Junias, my kinsmen, and my fellow prisoners, who are outstanding among the apostles, who also were in Christ before me."* In this passage Paul identifies two

> *"History teaches us that a revolution can only grow and spread as fast as it can reproduce leaders."*

additional and not-previously-known apostles, both of whom preceded him in the faith. And Junia was apparently a woman.[17] Gender is NOT an obstacle to organic house church leadership! I believe it is biblical to say that if you are qualified to lead a family, then you are probably qualified to lead a house church, irrespective of gender.

---

[17]See Dr. James Edwards, **Romans**, New International Biblical Commentary Series, Vol. 6 (Peabody: Hendrickson Publishers, 1992). *"Depending on the Greek accenting of Iounia (a form of the name which unfortunately obscures its gender), the name could be either male (Junias) or female (Junia). The name is normally presumed male, but a recent study reveals over 250 examples of it in Greek literature, not one of which is masculine! This seems to be nearly incontrovertible evidence that the name is feminine . . ."* Page 355.

# Who's In Charge Here, Anyway?

History teaches us that a revolution can only grow and spread as fast as it can reproduce leaders. The New Testament Church spread and grew at an amazingly rapid pace, due in no small part to the fact that the early Church understood the boundaries and qualifications for leadership to be broad and inclusive, as opposed to narrow and exclusive. In other words, they understood that God desires you to be a leader in the Church that meets in your house unless there is a specific reason why you should not (i.e., a specific unrepented violation of the leadership qualities found in 1 Timothy 3:1-13).

## What Leadership Looks Like In Your House Church

How leadership manifests itself in your organic house church will vary, hopefully within the guidelines provided by Scripture. I know of organic house churches where each meeting is facilitated by a different person or family, and other fellowships where there are recognized elders. But remember, generally speaking, the New Testament pattern is that house churches get started and then produce leaders, not the other way around. For now, practice being the Church of Nike: *Just Do It!*

*Reflection Question #1 -* What (if anything) did you learn from this chapter about organic house church leadership that you did not know before.

# Safe Houses of Hope And Prayer

**Reflection Question #2 -** How important are you in your house church? In other words, could anyone in your house church reproduce what you do, or is it unique to you and you alone? How could you change that?

**Reflection Question #3 -** What did you learn about the role of women in organic house church leadership? Do you agree or disagree? Why or Why not?

# Chapter 8

## Leadership Gifts And Mending Nets

Consider the following story a parable on leadership. We'll cal it *"The Parable Of The Shipwreck."*

***Shipwreck!*** *Leadership Lessons I Learned While Swimming To Shore*

It was a beautiful day when I went down to the seashore to enjoy the sunshine and read my book. I had scarcely gotten situated in a comfortable beach chair and had begun reading when I noticed it. Out on the horizon where the ocean met the sky I saw the outline of a ship. As the minutes ticked away it grew larger as it moved slowly towards shore. As it drew closer to shore it quickly became apparent that the ship was in trouble. It was sinking and people were jumping ship and swimming for shore. That's when I saw them.

It was obvious that I wasn't going to get to read my book, so I put it away and began watching as people from the sinking ship began coming ashore. The first person to emerge from the water had a dignified look about him. He wrung water from his drenched clothes, took a deep breath and began walking toward me. *"Well, that was interesting,"* he said as he came up to me. *"At least we were close to shore. The last time that happened to me I floated around for three days before someone finally picked me up,"* he said matter-of-factly with a slight hint of a grin on his face. *"You wouldn't happen to know where I could rent another boat, would you.*

# Safe Houses of Hope And Prayer

*This has put us behind schedule and I really would like to get moving again as quickly as possible,"* he said, sounding somewhat irritated at the whole affair.

I was still trying to take it all in when the second person out of the water came up to join us. He was more animated and excited than the first fellow, with a glint of wildness in his eyes that made me wonder what was coming next. *"Wow!"* he exclaimed as he grabbed the first fellow by the shoulders and spun him around to look him in the eyes. *"Wasn't that amazing! And it happened exactly the way He told me it would - the storm, the shipwreck, you at the helm, us swimming to shore . . . the whole thing! Isn't God amazing!"* he declared. And without giving anyone a chance to respond, he continued on, *"And as I was swimming to shore I heard Him say that it's going to be O.K., and that we are going to find another boat and make it safely to where we're headed. God is so amazing!"*

As all of this was going on a crowd of on-lookers began gathering, some talking to us and others watching the ship slip beneath the waves offshore. That was when the third survivor approached us and greeted the other two. It was obvious by now that they were all friends and traveling together. *"Hey, guys,"* he said with a hint of mischievousness in his voice. *"There's a crowd starting to gather around here. You never know when we'll have another chance like this. Maybe I should say something to everyone about how God just spared our lives and how they should trust Him, too!"*

The third man had scarcely gotten the words out when a fourth man from the ship joined their company. He had a concerned look on his face as he asked the other three,

# Leadership Gifts And Mending Nets

*"Fellas, has anyone done a head count yet? Are we sure everyone made it off the boat O.K.? Maybe we should form a search party and make certain everyone is accounted for. I wouldn't want to lose anyone just because we weren't paying attention. Besides, some of them may be injured and need help."*

A fifth and final man now joined his four companions, carrying a bundle under his arm. *"Don't tell me you actually swam to shore carrying those things,"* one of the four chided him. *"Hey, these are rare, out of print books,"* he responded indignantly. *"I'll toss you overboard before I leave these babies behind,"* he declared triumphantly, but with a smile. *"And before I go anywhere with you four characters again I want to see the operating manual for the new boat. I may even do a safety training class for everyone before we sail. Better safe than sorry."*

As the five traveling companions walked away, talking and teasing each other, I learned an important lesson: Be careful who you travel with. You may have to swim to shore with them later.

## Leaders, Gifts And Mending Nets

*"And He gave some as apostles, and some as prophets, and some as evangelists, and some as pastors and teachers, for **the equipping** of the saints for the work of service, to the building up of the body of Christ; until we all attain to the unity of the faith, and of the knowledge of the Son of God, to a mature man, to the measure of the stature which belongs to the fulness of Christ."* (Ephesians 4:11-13)

# Safe Houses of Hope And Prayer

O.K., it's time to interpret the *"Parable Of The Shipwreck"* and to do it in terms of the 5-fold leadership gifts we discover in Ephesians 4:11ff. There Paul lists the five leadership gifts/callings

> *"Paul tells us the reason and purpose for these five leadership gifts: to equip fellow believers for the work of the ministry."*

which Jesus gave to His Church following His resurrection and ascension: Apostles, Prophets, Evangelists, Pastors and Teachers. And just as important, Paul tells us the reason and purpose for these five leadership gifts: to equip fellow believers for the work of the ministry.

Now, before we interpret the parable (as my daughter would say, *"Wait for it, dad, wait for it"*) I want to comment on this word "equip," found in Ephesians 4:12. The Greek word (_katartidzo_) has a long history. Its root meaning is

> *"The highest and primary calling of a gifted biblical leader is to model, teach and assist others in the art of mending their nets."*

the idea of restoration. In Classical Greek it was used to describe restoring the mentally ill to health, and of fishermen mending their nets. Jesus Himself grew up on the shores of the Sea of Galilee, as did several of His disciples. Many times throughout His life He had undoubtedly watched fishermen dry, mend and fold their nets. Two of His disciples, John and James, were in the process of drying and mending their nets when Jesus called them to follow Him (Matthew 4:21-22, Mark 1:19-20).

# Leadership Gifts And Mending Nets

You can learn a lot about leadership from a net. There is an important spiritual lesson here which Jesus, His disciples and the Apostle Paul understood very well. You can't fish with broken nets. And that includes fishing for men. The highest and primary calling of a gifted biblical leader is to model, teach and assist others in the art of mending their nets. A gifted leader, manifesting a Jesus-shaped spirituality, is a mender of nets.

O.K., lets go back to our *Parable*. Have you figured it out? Understand the parable of the shipwreck.

**The first person off the sinking ship was the Apostle.** The Apostolic gift tends to be a pioneering, ground-breaking gift. This person is very focused on the health and mission of the Church. Apostolic people don't let a little thing like a sinking ship deter them from their goal of taking the Kingdom of God to places where it hasn't

> *"The Apostolic gift 'mends' the church's nets by keeping it forward-focused and on mission."*

been before. They are people who can *"see far"* into where God is going, who understand the implications of what they see, and can formulate the strategies necessary to get there. They are disturbers of the status quo who are always pushing the church forward in its mission. The Apostolic gift mends the church's nets by keeping it forward-focused and on mission.

**The second person off the sinking ship was the Prophet.** The Prophetic gift *"hears clearly"* concerning God's heart and purposes for His Church. Prophets are the Church's eyes and ears and bring fresh spiritual insights into the purposes of God for His people. For reasons the Scriptures never fully explain, God's plan is for Apostles and Prophets to work closely together in the task of establishing spiritual foundations for the building of the Church,

*"So then you are no longer strangers and aliens, but you are fellow citizens with the saints, and are of God's household, having been built upon* **the foundation of the apostles and prophets**, *Christ Jesus Himself being the corner stone, in whom the whole building, being fitted together is growing into a holy temple in the Lord; in whom you also are being built together into a dwelling of God in the Spirit."* (Ephesians 2:19-22).

Without the focus and strategies of the Apostolic gift, Prophets become prophetic junkies addicted to fresh words and visions. Churches left in the hands of the Prophetic gift become centers of spiritual adrenaline, always listening, always seeking a fresh word from God, but never moving forward in the mission of the Church. Such groups end up chasing their prophetic tails with no plan or strategy to implement what they are hearing.

*"The Prophetic gift mends the church's nets by bringing fresh spiritual insights into the purposes of God for His*

But without the Prophetic voice, Apostles become builders of Apostolic empires, seeking to implement grand strategies with no prophetic clarity for what God is seeking to accomplish. Together, Prophets hear God's heart for people and places while Apostles keep the church focused on its greater mission and the strategies needed for planting house church networks to reach those people and places. Apostles see far and understand implications. Prophets hear clearly and have insight into God's heart. Apostles are about strategy and architecture. Prophets are about vision and adrenaline. The Prophetic gift mends the church's nets by bringing fresh spiritual insights into the purposes of God for His people.

*The third person off the sinking ship was the Evangelist.*
The Evangelist is the one who *"sees opportunity,"* specifically the opportunity to bring more sheep into the fold. In the book of Acts, Philip of Caesarea was known as Philip, the Evangelist. After hearing from the Lord, Philip both saw and took advantage of the opportunity to share the gospel with an Ethiopian court official in Acts 21:8. Evangelists are the gatherers of stray sheep. Their passion is to

> *"The Evangelistic gift mends the Church's nets by focusing the Church's attention and message outward towards unbelievers who need to hear about Jesus."*

bring in large numbers of sheep, to see as many people brought into and involved with the church as possible. They are all about encouraging the church to turn both its thinking and its message outward and to seize opportunities to share the gospel.

But evangelists tend to live on adrenaline and activity. A

church built on or by an evangelist will be a hub of non-stop activity and programs. It will be very wide, but very shallow, with virtually every message being a salvation message, characterized by little depth or discipleship. The Evangelistic gift mends the Church's nets by focusing the Church's attention and message outward towards unbelievers who need to hear about Jesus.

**The fourth person off the sinking ship was the Pastor or Shepherd.** The English word "pastor" is actually the Greek word _poimen_ or "shepherd." The Pastoral gift is all about the sheep, and pastors are shepherds who simply love sheep. Pastors are relational people who want to spend time with the sheep. For them, ministry is all about meeting the needs of the sheep. Pastors are the networkers of the body, the counselors of the wounded and needy, the team and community builders who bring the body together.

> _"The Pastoral gift mends the church's nets by caring for the on-going personal needs of the sheep and promoting the healthy body-life of the Church."_

They live to see the body function together as an extended family. But if a church is left in the hands of the pastoral gift it will become a _need driven_ (as opposed to God-vision driven) counseling and rehab ministry, a spiritual hospital for the wounded that will soon be overwhelmed by endless needs. It will eventually come to resent and oppose the apostolic, prophetic and evangelistic gifts as disturbers of the status quo (In the immortal words of Ahab, _"Is this you, you troubler of Israel?"_). The Pastoral gift mends the church's nets by caring for the on-going personal needs of the sheep and promoting the healthy body-life of the Church.

***The fifth person off the sinking ship was the Teacher.***
Teachers *"dig deep"* and have understanding. Teachers have the ability to take complex biblical truth and to simplify it for the Church to understand. Teachers do not lay foundations (the task given to Apostles and Prophets) but they can explain foundations brilliantly! They are the explainers and apologists of the body. While Apostles have strategies for accomplishing God's purpose and Prophets have insight into God's purposes, Teachers look for understanding by digging deep into God's word in order to explain God's purposes. The role of the teacher is not to balance the apostolic or prophetic, but to explain and expound on the biblical basis for what God is doing and saying through the Apostles and Prophets.

If a church is founded upon or built around a gifted Teacher (as many churches today are) people will end up with notebooks full of great notes and insights, but with no practical ability to apply all that they have learned. And because

*"The Teaching gift mend's the Church's nets by taking complex biblical truth and simplifying it for the church to understand."*

Teachers are not Pastors, the practical needs of the sheep will suffer. Many a teacher has been hired as a "Pastor" for his teaching ability and later fired for his lack of pastoral skills (go figure!). And devoid of any Apostolic or Prophetic insights the Church will lack any sense of God's Kingdom purposes and the strategies needed to accomplish them with no fresh prophetic sense of God's heart for His people. The Teaching gift mend's the Church's nets by taking complex biblical truth and simplifying it for the church to understand.

## Some Final Thoughts on Mending Nets

It is important to point out that the gifted 5-fold leaders of the Church are NOT competitors with each other. They are collaborators. There is no spiritual hierarchy at work here. Each is a first-among-equals. No one is

*"An absence of all five leadership gifts functioning and working together will result in a lack of maturity in the Church."*

preeminent, and no one is expendable. And all have been called to be fools and spectacles before both the world and the Church (See 1 Corinthians 4). But the Church needs the ministry of all five gifts working together if the body of Christ is to grow into *"a mature man"* (Ephesians 4:13). An absence of all five leadership gifts functioning and working together will result in a lack of maturity in the Church.

It is also important to remember that the greatest weakness of any gift always lurks in the shadow of its greatest strength. The amazing apostolic gifting of a Paul which enabled him to endure hardship, stoning, shipwreck and persecution to take the Gospel to the Gentiles, also produced the weakness of a *"spiritual myopia."* We see this *"spiritual myopia"* in Paul's treatment of John Mark whom Paul kicked to the curb at the outset of the second missionary journey because John Mark

# Leadership Gifts And Mending Nets

had abandoned them on the first missionary journey. Paul's apostolic focus wouldn't allow him to see how John Mark would be an asset on any future journey. It took the pastoral gifting of Barnabas (whom

*". . . remember that the greatest weakness of any gift always lurks in the shadow of its greatest strength."*

the Church had nick-named *"Son of Encouragement"*) to take John Mark under his care and to disciple him. John Mark would eventually find his gift and write the Gospel According to Mark. Not bad for a missionary washout who was really a 5-Fold teacher-in-the-making.

Before we end our discussion of house church leadership and mending nets, I wanted to look at three more Scriptures and make some observations.

*"Now I exhort you, brethren, by the name of our Lord Jesus Christ, that you all agree, and there be no divisions among you, but you **be made complete** in the same mind and in the same judgment."* (1 Corinthians 1:10, NASB)

This passage is about divisions and unity in the Church. That would include your house church. Because there are people in your house church, you will have conflicts, even

*"When house churches and their leaders mend nets together as a team the result is unity."*

divisions. As Charlie Brown once observed: *"Mankind I love, it's people I can't stand"*. Paul's solution to divisions in the church is to be mended together (yep, same Greek word here for mending nets). Nothing heals divisions and builds unity better than the body and its leaders coming together in the common task of mending one another's nets. When house churches and their leaders mend nets together as a team the result is unity.

*"Brothers, if anyone is caught in any transgression, you who are spiritual should* **restore** *him in a spirit of gentleness. Keep watch on yourself, lest you too be tempted."* (Galatians 6:1)

What stands out to me here is that the emphasis is not upon the trespass, but upon the importance of manifesting a spirit of gentleness (i.e., humility) in the process of restoration (yep, _katartidzo_). Life is messy (if in doubt, read Chapter 5). Stuff happens. People are going to stumble (literally, *"be overtaken before one has the opportunity to flee"* - the meaning of the word "caught"). The call of biblical leadership is to manifest a spirit of genuine personal humility (*"that could have been me"*) as we restore that person by helping them to mend the broken nets of their lives. Remember, next time it may be YOUR nets that are broken!

*"For what thanks can we render to God for you in return for all the joy with which we rejoice before our God on your account, as we night and day keep praying most earnestly that we may see your face, and* **may complete** *what is lacking in your faith?"* (1 Thessalonians 3:9-10, NASB)

Paul understood that net mending is a team activity. He longed to be with the believers in Thessalonica so that he

# Leadership Gifts And Mending Nets

could have a part in making them complete (i.e., helping them mend their nets). Paul understood that we all need the ministry of other people with other gifts and callings in

*"We will never be "complete" without one another."*

our lives to mend our nets and to make up what is lacking in our faith. We will never be "complete" without one another.

*"Now may the God of peace who brought again from the dead our Lord Jesus, the great shepherd of the sheep, by the blood of the eternal covenant, **equip** you with everything good that you may do his will, working in us that which is pleasing in his sight, through Jesus Christ, to whom be glory forever and ever. Amen."* (Hebrews 13:20-21)

The author of Hebrews saw that, ultimately, it is God-in-Christ Who mends our broken nets in order to equip and perfect us. But while it is God Himself Who mends the broken and torn nets of our lives, He usually does it through the gifts and the people He has appointed in the body of Christ.

## Shredding, Mending and House Church

Life in this fallen, sin ravaged world shreds the nets of people's lives. And that includes you, me and the people in our house churches. The good news is that in the Kingdom of God, and that small manifestation of it that meets in your house, God has placed gifted leaders whose calling, purpose and function is to help God's people mend the broken nets of their lives, and to enable all of us to get back to our original calling: to fish for men. We can't fish with broken nets.

# Safe Houses of Hope And Prayer

**Reflection Question #1 -** What did you learn from *"The Parable Of The Shipwreck"* regarding Scriptural leadership gifts that you did not know before?

**Reflection Question #2 -** Like nearly all spiritual gifts, the leadership gifts of Ephesians 4 are generally known by how they function. Do you see yourself walking in one of the five leadership gifts, and if so, *"how's it working for you,"* particularly in the eyes of those around you?

**Reflection Question #3 -** We observed earlier that *"the greatest weakness of any gift always lurks in the shadow of its greatest strength."* How does this apply to you?

What is your greatest strength (spiritual gift)?

What is your greatest weakness in relation to your gift?

# Chapter 9

## When You Gather Together

During times of historic spiritual awakening the move of God's Spirit re-organizes our plans and priorities, and dictates when and where things will happen. Old categories get swept away in the flood-tide of God's Spirit. In the Awakening of 1857 which broke out in New York, prayer gatherings such as the Fulton Street Prayer Meeting began in a few churches, but things quickly overflowed into area theaters and other locations, and were led by lay people (as opposed to professional, ordained clergy). If you weren't flexible, you would have looked and felt like a religious square peg surrounded by spiritual round holes!

In this Chapter I want to address a few of the more common practical issues which tend to arise as people begin their journey into organic house church and *Safe Houses of Hope and Prayer*. A flexible approach to these issues will work in your favor as the coming season of spiritual outpouring gets underway and challenges traditional ways of doing things, presenting you and your house church with an increasing need for flexibility.

### When and Where To Meet

I grew up in the American South where, throughout my childhood, we had Blue Laws. A Blue Law was a local ordinance declaring Sunday to be a commercial-free day. Simply put, it legally meant that on Sundays all commercial establishments, from grocery stores to gas stations, were

# Safe Houses of Hope And Prayer

closed and most people went to Church (and the ones who didn't go always knew that they should have gone!). My how things have changed. When it comes to the times and places of our house church meetings today, you and I have the luxury of freedom of choice.

I recently read an article about Christians in China. The article described how, at the end of a busy workday, a group of 30 believers met on one of the highest floors of a Beijing office tower. The location of the meeting was a secret until that very day with the time and place being confirmed with brief cell phone calls and exchanged passwords to protect privacy. As rush traffic filled the streets below, this group of 30 Chinese working professionals began to pray and to worship God clandestinely. Welcome to organic (and underground) house church, Chinese style. Here are believers who are simply thankful to be able to meet. They don't spend a lot of time quibbling about the day, time, and place. They have learned to *"Just Do It!"*

## What About The Sabbath?

Whenever this topic of when to meet is discussed, there is nearly always someone who believes that Church must take place on the Sabbath. We refer to these folk as *"Sabbatarians"* and they generally have a problem with this idea of meeting anytime. While my first tendency is to label the whole discussion another square peg versus round hole episode, I try to resist that urge and offer four specific biblical responses instead (after which I move on, reminding myself that religious square pegs can stare at spiritual round holes all day without ever understanding the problem).

## When You Gather Together

**First**, the early church didn't worship on the Sabbath (the seventh day of the week, or our Saturday). Rather, they met on the first day of the week (our Sunday), because they understood that the death and resurrection of Jesus had altered the times and seasons.

**Second**, the Council of Elders in Acts 15, which took up the controversial question of whether Gentile (non-Jewish)converts to Christianity needed to keep the Law of Moses (which would include the Sabbath), answered with a resounding *"No!"* They did not regard or require Sabbath observance as necessary for either Jewish or non-Jewish converts.

**Third**, Paul, writing to the predominantly Gentile church at Colossae (present day Western Asia Minor or Turkey) told those Gentile believers not to allow anyone to *"act as your judge in regard to food or drink or in respect to a festival or a new moon or a Sabbath day, things which are a mere shadow of what is to come; but the substance belongs to Christ."* (Colossians 2:16-17).

This admonition would only make sense if Jewish religious square pegs were attempting to impose the Old Testament Law of Sabbath-keeping on Gentile believers as something necessary for their faith and

*"No one goes back to the type or shadow when they have the substance and fulfillment through faith in Christ."*

obedience. Indeed, the book of Hebrews teaches that the Old Testament Sabbath as a day of rest was a type and shadow

## Safe Houses of Hope And Prayer

of the "rest of faith" which the believer enters into by faith in Christ (see Hebrews 4:1-10). No one goes back to the type or shadow when they have the substance and fulfillment through faith in Christ.

**Fourth**, if Christians are obligated to *"Remember the Sabbath day, to keep it holy"* (as required by the Old Testament Law) then they are **also** obligated to keep the other 612 requirements of the Law of Moses. Obedience to the Law is an all-or-nothing deal. We don't get to pick and choose

> *"Organic house church can take place literally any where on any day and at any time."*

which ones we will keep and which we won't. And to be guilty of breaking one Law is to be guilty of breaking them ALL. Or have you not read the book of Galatians (Or Chapter 5 of this book where we talk about legalism versus transformation)?

Organic house church can take place literally any where on any day and at any time. We actually see this occurring in the Book of Acts in the early church. There we learn that the early church met *"**day by day** continuing with one mind in the temple, and breaking bread from **house to house** . . ."* (See Acts 2:46). Gone is the notion that we must go to a holy place on a holy day to hear a holy person lecture on holy things. When and where your *Safe House of Hope And Prayer* meets is up to you and those in your group. It could meet during the week, or, yes, even on Sunday. It may meet in one fixed location or you may choose to move around *"from house to house"* as the early Church did. So choose a time and a place, make certain that everyone in your group

# When You Gather Together

knows about it, and then *"Just Do It"!*

## Is That A "Bulletin" Or A Pre-Printed Rut?

I have often mused that a trained and experienced pastor could go into nearly any protestant Church in America on short notice and lead it, beginning with the Sunday Service. Why? Because with only a few genuine variations their services are all basically the same. Most of what I would need to know to lead the service would be found in the pre-printed bulletin (or in the PowerPoint on the screen). The first week might be awkward, as I learned the idiosyncracies of the other staff and participants, but in a couple of weeks most things would return to normal (By the way, such itinerant pastors do exist. They're called interim pastors and, yes, I've been one. Long story. No time here.).

And I'm not alone in this view, as I discovered when I read *Jim And Casper Go To Church*.[18] Imagine an atheist and an evangelical pastor visiting 15 of the top evangelical churches in America and critiquing them (I heard Matt Casper speak at a Conference in Ontario, California and it was an eye-opening experience). Among their many observations, Jim Henderson (the atheist) commented on how similar all of the services were. In Church-speak that's called a familiar *"order of service."* In street vernacular it's called being in a rut.

---

[18]Jim Henderson and Matt Casper, *Jim and Casper Go to Church: Frank Conversation about Faith, Churches, and Well-Meaning Christians* (Ventura, CA: Barna Books, 2007).

# Safe Houses of Hope And Prayer

It is not the goal of *Safe Houses of Hope and Prayer* to belittle old institutional ruts, or to create all-new organic house church ruts. And this is why organic house church people who have been at this a while are often reluctant to answer the question, *"What should we do when we get together?"* It isn't that we don't have an answer. It's that we know any answer we give runs the two-fold risk of missing what God wants to do in your unique situation, and of starting you and your house church down the path of digging a new religious rut.

***Just remember:*** Regular behaviors quickly become predictable patterns; predictable patterns quickly become new traditions; new traditions quickly become old ruts, and old ruts quickly become graves with the ends knocked out. And who wants to attend Church in a grave?!

*"Every week may be different depending on what has transpired in people's lives during the week."*

## So, What Should We Do When We Meet?

So, what should you do when you meet? Well, I wouldn't suggest sitting around and staring at each other (just in case you were wondering)! But throughout this book we have tried to illustrate some of the diversity among organic house churches and to make the point that there's no one way to do organic house church - no set order of things. Every week may be different depending on what has transpired in people's lives during the week. This means that you need to

## When You Gather Together

be sensitive to the voice of God and the leading of the Holy Spirit (after all, it's His meeting. Right?). So, be sensitive and flexible. When I first started doing house church I would come with an extensive bible study syllabus of things to

*"A religion-shaped spirituality asks, 'What's on the agenda' . . . . A Jesus-shaped spirituality asks 'What's on God's heart for this gathering'."*

teach (notes, handouts, the whole works!). That way, if the Lord failed to show up I would always be ready to bail Him out and lead the meeting! Needless to say, I don't do that anymore - and neither should you!

And this helps to point out one of the primary differences between a religion-shaped spirituality and a Jesus-shaped spirituality when it comes to church. A religion-shaped spirituality asks, *"What's on the agenda"* (or its equivalent, *"What's in the bulletin?"*). A Jesus-shaped spirituality asks *"What's on God's heart for this gathering."* Do you appreciate the difference between these two questions? The answer to one of those questions can be pre-printed in a bulletin. The answer to the other can only be discovered as the worshiping Church enters in to seek God in the moment.

This question of *"What should we do"* highlights the fact that when we gather together as the Church, we engage in four basic activities: worship, community-building, net-mending and outreach. As you work on planning your unique gathering ask yourself these four basic questions:

1. What are we doing to worship God?

# Safe Houses of Hope And Prayer

2. What are we doing to build community with one another?

3. What are we doing to mend one another's nets by exercising the gifts He has given us?

4. What are we doing to reach out to others beyond our immediate fellowship?

**Some Time Tested Components**

Here are some basic time tested components of organic house church that are worth considering:

*Food And Fellowship* - Learn to eat together and to just hang out together. Students of church history like to point out that during the Protestant Reformation, Martin Luther would entertain his students over dinner and engage in significant theological discussions during the meal.[19] Meals can be great social occasions where people can let down their guard and get to know others. Meals can help to put new people at ease. Shared meals are an excellent way to begin building community together, and pot lucks (everyone bring something) are a good way to do this.

*Worship And Prayer* - Learn to worship together. Invite people to bring their favorite worship CDs or musical instruments. Make a joyful noise! Learn to pray and to wait in silence on the Lord. American Christians tend to fear silence.

---

[19]Luther, Martin. *Tabletalk: Luther's Comments on Life, the Church and the Bible.* Geanies House, Fearn, Ross-Shire Tain GBR: Christian Focus Publications, 2003.

## When You Gather Together

But prolonged silence is often what is needed to hear the still small voice of the Holy Spirit. As your house church assembles and begins to worship, take time to seek the face of God in prayer, waiting to

> *"Spiritual gifts are best identified by their exercise as the Church ministers to one another, and that requires some time and practice."*

see if He has something to say to the waiting, listening Church. Don't fear the silence of God's Presence (by trying to fill it with prayer verbiage). Use the silence of God's Presence as an opportunity to hear the voice of the Holy Spirit. Then, be prepared step out in faith to pray for one another, to prophesy over one another, to share words of encouragement with one another, to share a psalm, a hymn or a spiritual song. Be willing to take a risk that God is actually speaking and moving among His Church.

*Personal Ministry -* As you worship and pray and wait upon the Lord, invite the Holy Spirit to come and anoint all of the gifts He has sovereignly placed in the body. Ask the Holy Spirit to cause His gifts to surface as your house church ministers to one another. Spiritual gifts are best identified by their exercise as the Church ministers to one another, and that requires some time and practice, not to mention a certain amount of love and patience! And God's anointed leaders are best identified by the gifts they exercise in the body over time.

Ask people for their needs *("where are your nets broken tonight")* and then take the initiative to pray for them. We often set a chair in the center of the room (we call it the hot

# Safe Houses of Hope And Prayer

seat), ask the person being prayed for to sit there while those who feel led to pray lay hands on the individual and pray for them. We

> *"Everyone is allowed to share, but no one is allowed to dominate."*

encourage those praying to share what they are hearing and seeing from the Lord for that person. We've seen amazing things happen as we have worshiped and prayed for needs this way.

**Open Participation -** Everyone is allowed to share, but no one is allowed to dominate. If needed, implement a 5-Minute Rule. Anyone can share anything that's on their heart, but it must be limited to 5 minutes unless the group agrees to allow more time and there is no one else who wants to share.

**Bible Study/Teaching -** Simple house church isn't another Bible study club, but that doesn't mean we don't study or teach the bible. The goal is to find balance between bible teaching and the other equally important parts of simple church. This can be as simple as reading passages of Scripture and sharing a devotional you read during the week, or as complex as someone leading the Church in a detailed study of a biblical book or a topic.[20]

---

[20]At the risk of seeming self-promoting, allow me to offer a couple of suggestions. **First,** our book **When Jesus Visits His Church** is designed to be a multi-week study of the Seven Churches of Asia in the book of Revelation, appropriate for short-term use in a house church setting. **Second**, our book on discipleship, **And They Dreamt Of A Kingdom**, offers 42 lessons on discipleship which can be used as weekly lessons in an organic house church setting.

# When You Gather Together

*Simplicity -* Remember that people in your *Safe House of Hope and Prayer* will model what they see and experience. So K.I.S.S. up (Keep It Simple Stupid)!

## Building Community With B.E.L.L.S.

There are many ways to build community, but they do not need to be complicated. In fact, simple is better. Here's one simple idea called "BELLS." B.E.L.L.S. is an acronym which stands for five simple activities designed to build community because everyone in the group agress to practice them. Here they are:

**B**less - Each person agrees to find three people this week and to bless them by doing an act of kindness for them.
**E**at - Each person agrees to share a meal or a cup of coffee with three people this week.
**L**earn - Each person agrees that in their devotional life they will learn one new thing from God and be prepared to briefly share it with others when you meet.
**L**isten - Each person agrees to spend one hour this week alone with God praying, listening to His voice and recording what they hear.
**S**end - As an organic house church you recognize that you have been sent by God to those around you to introduce them to the Kingdom of God.

Just by practicing these five simple community-building disciplines and then gathering together to share your experiences and to worship together, you can take a powerful step toward becoming a genuine community of believers with obedience to Jesus at your center.

# Safe Houses of Hope And Prayer

## The Challenges of Legalism and Reproducibility

The challenge with offering more specific things to do is the danger we run of taking biblical models (*"The New Testament Church did 'A' and God did 'B'"*), turning those models into methods

> *"Revolutionary leaders work to set people up for success in their absence."* - George Barna

(*"We should do 'A' if we want God to do 'B'"*) which eventually become formulas (*"If you do 'A' God will always do 'B'"*). Spiritual freedom is a scary thing for many people who prefer being told what to do, along with when and how to do it. Any legalistic adherence to anything will eventually quench a movement of God's Spirit.

Whatever you do, work to keep one important principle in the forefront of your mind: **Reproducibility**. Let me say it this way. Avoid doing things which people in your simple house church cannot reproduce on their own. The more complicated the model, the greater the likelihood of failure when others try to reproduce it.

George Barna, speaking on the characteristics of revolutionary leaders, once observed that *revolutionary leaders work to set people up for success in their absence.* Will the house churches you start fail in your absence because the model you gave them was too complicated (or too personalized around you) for them to reproduce without you? If so, then don't do it. If the model you give people is dependent upon you (or someone else like an "apostolic house church planter") then you are setting people up for failure in your absence. Whatever you do when you get together should be simple enough to model and reproduce. In order to be successful in the long-run, organic house church must be simple and reproducible.

***Reflection Question #1*** - What did you learn from this Chapter about what organic house churches should do when they meet? Did the discussion meet your expectations?

***Reflection Question #2*** - What additional questions do you have which did not get answered?

***Reflection Question #3*** - What is the potential danger in giving people a model of organic house church to follow?

# Safe Houses of Hope And Prayer

# Chapter 10

## That's Almost Music!

My wife and I were privileged to attend one of the last conferences conducted by John Wimber, founder of the Association of Vineyard Churches, before he went home to be with the Lord. Before his conversion to Christ John had been a professional musician and the road manager for a very successful and well-known vocal group. John never lost his passion for music and the Vineyard movement became a pioneer in the area of contemporary Christian worship music.

At this particular conference the session began with a time of singing and worship led by a worship band that, well, still needed some work. At the end, as the band was putting away its instruments and John was taking his place behind the podium, preparing to speak, he turned to the band members and said, *"Thanks fellows, that was almost music."* I laughed so hard I thought I would split a seam! John had summed up the essence of the moment, and had unknowingly highlighted a problem in the contemporary Church. We are no longer satisfied with *"almost music."*

### A Singing People

The people of God have always been a singing people. The Psalms of David were originally sung, and on occasion it was the worship choir that led the way into battle (see 2 Chronicles 20:21ff). Jesus sang hymns with his disciples at the last supper (see Matt. 26:30; Mark 14:26). In the early

# Safe Houses of Hope And Prayer

Second Century A.D., the Roman Governor of Bythinia (Asia Minor), Pliny the Elder, described to the Roman Emperor Trajan how the early Christians would gathered together and *"sing responsively a hymn to Christ as to a god."*

During the dark times of the Middle Ages, as Europe reeled under barbarian invasions and civilization teetered on the brink of collapse, the Church developed the Gregorian Chant as the disciplined music for difficult times. During the Protestant Reformation, reformers like Martin Luther wrote new songs to celebrate a new found faith, and the Gregorian Chant of the Medieval Church gave way to the strains of the Psalter and a rediscovery of the Psalms set to music.

Times of revival have always produced new hymns and songs. During the Evangelical Awakening of the 1700s in England, one of the most prolific of hymn writers of his day was Charles Wesley who wrote some 4,000 hymns. Charles Wesley wrote new hymns for specific Methodist congregations to encourage them during dark times of persecution, or to celebrate times of spiritual victories. The songs of their worship were directly related to their spiritual life-experiences.

During the Great Manhattan Prayer Revival of 1857-58, two prominent leaders of the revival at Jayne's Hall (in Philadelphia) were the Reverend Dudley Tyng, an Episcopal, and the Reverend George Duffield, a Presbyterian. In May of 1858 Dudley Tyng was mortally wounded in an accident. On his death-bed Tyng told his father to tell the men in Jayne's Hall *"to stand up for Jesus."* When Tyng's father related this story at his son's memorial service, George Duffield was so moved by the dying words of his friend that he went home

# That's Almost Music

and wrote the hymn we sing today, *"Stand up, Stand up for Jesus, ye soldiers of the cross."*

The Welsh Revival of 1904 came to be known as "the singing revival" because of the prominent place given to corporate worship through the singing of great old Welsh hymns. Whether in times of crisis, times of revival, or times of regular worship, the people of God have always been a singing people. Historically, Christian singing and worship has nearly always been related to the Church's life-experience with God. Through their music the people of God worshiped the same God whom they worshiped with daily their lives.

## Cheap Worship

The relationship between music and worship and personal Christian experience has been complicated in our Postmodern culture by the rise of the phenomenon known as contemporary Christian music, which has now become a multi-million

*"Contemporary Western Christianity excels at what can best be described as cheap worship, a form of worship that doesn't cost us anything."*

dollar industry (owned almost wholly by secular entertainment companies). It is a phenomenon that has turned worship into a consumer item and contemporary church-goers into a market of Christian consumers. The popularity of this new commercial genre of consumer-driven Christian music has confronted God's people with a new challenge that affects how we do church. Specifically, it is confronting the Church with the challenge of cheap worship. Contemporary Western Christianity excels at what can best be described as cheap worship, a form of worship that doesn't cost us anything. We go to church, the worship band fires up, we sing half-a-dozen or so contemporary worship songs, listen to somebody else speak and pray and call it good. No muss, no fuss, no cost. We've worshiped God, had a nice emotional experience and it didn't cost us a thing. And you don't even need to be a believer to engage in this cheap worship.

### King David, the Psalmist, Understood

While working on this Chapter I was reminded of the incident involving King David in 2 Samuel 24. In order to stop the plague which was ravaging the land due to David's disobedience in ordering a census, the prophet Gad told David to build an altar on the threshing floor owned by Araunah the Jebusite. Listen to the conversation between David and Araunah:

*"And Araunah said, 'Why has my lord the king come to his servant?' David said, 'To buy the threshing floor from you, in order to build an altar to the LORD, that the plague may be averted from the people' Then Araunah said to David, 'Let my lord the king take and offer up what seems good to him. Here are the oxen for the burnt offering and the threshing sledges and the yokes of the oxen for the wood. All this, O king, Araunah gives to the king.' And Araunah said to the king, 'May the LORD your God accept you.' But the king said to Araunah, 'No, but I will buy it from you for a price. I will not offer burnt offerings to the LORD my God that cost me nothing.' So David bought the threshing floor and the oxen*

# That's Almost Music

*for fifty shekels of silver."* (2 Samuel 24:21-24)

The purpose of building the altar on that spot was to worship God, to confess his disobedience and to seek God's favor to stop the plague. Wanting to help do the right thing,

> *"Spiritual lessons which cost us nothing are generally worth what we pay for them."*

Araunah offered the spot for free (cheap worship). David refused the offer. Why? I believe it was because David understood something about the importance of sacrificial worship - worship that costs us something.

Spiritual lessons which cost us nothing are generally worth what we pay for them. They are quickly forgotten, as is cheap worship. Worship is cheap when it focuses upon us, rather than upon God. Worship is cheap when its purpose is to bless us, rather than to bless God. Worship is cheap when it focuses upon hearing ourselves sing our favorite song, rather than hearing God speak, even if it isn't what we want to hear. Worship is cheap when it consists of nothing more than singing a worship song that any unbeliever could sing without a clue that it describes a spiritual experience that is not theirs.

## Beware of Cheap Worship

The Moravian Church became legendary for its worship, its community, its commitment to prayer and its commitment to missions. The declaration of the first Moravian missionaries was *"May the Lamb that was slain receive the reward of His suffering."* This is the declaration of sacrificial worship, seldom heard in our churches today which have been overtaken by a wave of cheap worship. ***Beware of cheap worship.***

***Beware*** of worship that requires no price or sacrifice on the part of the individual in order to participate;

***Beware*** of worship that becomes a new formula for a predictable and successful worship experience, rather than an unpredictable divine event;

***Beware*** of worship that causes people to worship their worship because it has become the new formula for causing God to step into our presence, rather than challenging us to step into God's presence;

***Beware*** of worship that begins to look like a replica of the priests of Baal, dancing around the altar in order to *"make God come down"* (O.K., See 1 Kings 18:26ff).

### Baggage or Blessing?

Music and worship in organic house church can be a blessing, or it can be baggage. It depends on what we do with it. I have seen Christians argue and Churches split over the color of a new hymnal, or over which hymnal to use, or whether or not to use a hymnal versus song sheets. Religion-shaped spiritualities can be very inflexible about such things. Some Christians dislike contemporary worship music (*"I don't like the rhythm and they are theologically shallow"*) and prefer traditional hymns (*"Good theology and the music*

# That's Almost Music

doesn't drown out the words"), while other people will only sing from the Psalter Hymnal (the Psalms set to music, usually in minor keys just to make sure that you don't enjoy them too much!). Well, you get the picture. These conflicts can be manifestations of a religion-shaped spirituality which thinks it has found the spiritual formula for singing, worship and finding God's presence. A Jesus-shaped spirituality learns to worship in the moment without any expectation that a particular moment will ever repeat itself. It simply builds a temporary altar, worships in the moment, and then moves on.

O.K., it's time to shed our religious music baggage and start over. God is pleased with the worship and music of our hearts. Your house church will eventually learn to worship together, and in the process they will discover what style

> *"A Jesus-shaped spirituality learns to 'worship in the moment' without any expectation that a particular moment will ever repeat itself."*

of music meets the worship needs of those in your fellowship. Is there a musically inclined person who can play the piano or guitar to facilitate the music? If not, then you can do it *a capella* (without instruments) or you can purchase music CDs of your favorites hymns or songs and learn to sing along. But be flexible and creative. Learn to appreciate the diversity of music and worship in the body of Christ (because not everyone is like you . . . or me!). Remember the biblical standard for music and worship: *"Make a joyful noise to the Lord, all the earth"*! And you will never hear the Lord complain, *"that was almost music"*!

# Safe Houses of Hope And Prayer

## A Little Application There Maestro

***Rediscover Sacrificial Worship.*** I believe that the Church needs to recover a holistic view of worship by re-uniting the idea of worship with the biblical understanding of living a life of sacrificial obedience. I think we see this idea worship-thru-obedience illustrated in Genesis 22 where God told Abraham to sacrifice his son, Isaac (22:1-2). Now, listen to how Abraham described the situation to his servant, *"I and the lad will go yonder; and we will **worship** and return to you"* (22:5).

> *". . . a life of sacrificial obedience which personally costs us something is, itself, an act of worship before God."*

Did you get it? The required obedience which God described as a sacrifice - the sacrifice of Abraham's son, Isaac - Abraham described to his servant as worship. Welcome to sacrificial worship, worship which costs us something more than a few worship songs. In our organic house churches we need to model and teach the biblical truth that a life of sacrificial obedience which personally costs us something is, itself, an act of worship before God.

***Learn To Be Creative.*** Challenge your house church to come up with creative worship ideas that go beyond just singing songs. In one of our house church meetings a woman asked if she could do a worship dance the following week. *"Of course!"* I said, even though liturgical dance is *"not my cup of tea."* The next week she performed an absolutely

# That's Almost Music

beautiful worship dance set to music, and everyone was greatly blessed (including me and my "cup of tea")! Challenge those in your organic house church to find new expressions of worshiping God *"in Spirit and in truth."* At other times we have engaged in times of silent worship before God, interspersed with the spontaneous reading of Psalms and other Scriptures. Some organic house churches have even experimented with writing their own worship songs. Be Creative!


*Reflection Question #1 -* What did you learn from this Chapter about worship that you did not know before?


*Reflection Question # 2 -* How would you explain the difference between cheap worship and sacrificial worship? Can you think of times in your own spiritual journey when you have experienced each of these?

# Safe Houses of Hope And Prayer

# Chapter 11

## Becoming Legendary For Our Good Deeds

Not too long ago I had a long conversation with a Campus Crusade for Christ (now "Cru") staff person who at that time was working in China among college students. He was home raising financial support and we met over coffee at one of my favorite coffee haunt in north Spokane. Several things popped out at me during that conversation, but I want to focus on his answer to one particular question regarding the

> *"It makes no difference what you believe, if what you believe makes no difference."*

persecution of Christians in China. His response was enlightening. *"The authorities don't care what you believe. They only care what you practice,"* he observed. Believers in China, he noted, have a constitutional right to freedom of religion (freedom of belief), but **not** freedom of practice. Chinese believers can openly profess Christianity and openly read their Bibles, he told me. What they **cannot** do is meet in unauthorized gatherings such as prayer groups, Bible studies or house churches. Belief is one thing; practice is something else.

I was stunned by the reality that the Communist authorities in China understand a profound truth which seems to have escaped the attention of most Western Christians: *"It makes no difference what you believe, if what you believe makes no difference."* You might want to re-read that last statement and allow its full impact to settle in.

Here in the Postmodern West, our Postmodern Culture has pretty much written off traditional institutional Christianity as irrelevant for any practical purposes. Why? In large part it is because we believe a lot, but we practice very little. This presents us with a puzzling and disturbing comparison. Unable to stop people from thinking or believing, the Chinese government has simply forbidden Christians from living and/or expressing what they believe. Here in the Postmodern West, without any coercion from anyone, we have simply taught people that abstract belief is sufficient - it gets you into heaven, and what more could you want. Here in the West, we don't really need some government official to forbid us from living and/or expressing what we believe. Our church leaders have filled that role, providing us with church services which leave everyone feeling good but which don't go anywhere. It's enough to simply meet and believe. The Chinese authorities should take notes.

By now you're probably thinking that I'm being overly critical on this point, and there are certainly some notable exceptions to my observations. But before you reject my observations out-of-hand, you really should read *Jim And Casper Go To Church*.[21] One of the observations made by Matt Casper (the atheist) regarding nearly *every one* of the fifteen largest evangelical churches in America that they attended and analyzed was, *"When do you get around to*

---

[21] Jim Henderson and Matt Casper, *Jim and Casper Go to Church: Frank Conversation about Faith, Churches, and Well-Meaning Christians* (Ventura, CA: Barna Books, 2007).

*telling people to DO things?"* Allow me to quote from the book:

*"Casper simply could not imagine Jesus telling his followers that the most important thing they should be doing is holding church services. And yet this was the only logical conclusion he was able to come to based upon what he'd observed. If people who had never heard of Jesus wanted to see what Christians were most interested in, they would probably start their search in some of the same churches we visited. 'If that's where they started, they would have to conclude that Jesus' number one priority was that Christians invest the very best of their energy and their money into putting on a huge church service - a killer show, as it were,' said Casper. 'Jim, is this what Jesus told you guys to do?'"*

No, Casper, it isn't. But it is what we excel at. Cheap worship that costs us little, or nothing. Simply put, ideas without consequences and beliefs without practice are like salt that has become tasteless (Matthew 5:13). And our culture understands that:

*"It makes no difference what you believe, if what you believe makes no difference."*

### Making a Difference

I am convinced that one of the ways believers are to live out a faith which makes a difference is through our good deeds done in the name of Christ. Having given up on the institutional church, our Postmodern culture has concluded that it doesn't need Jesus to manifest good deeds. The Church, on the other hand, has concluded that it doesn't need good deeds to manifest Jesus. The world's plan seems to be working better than the Church's plan.

But I believe God wants to change this situation. As this unfolding move of God's Spirit in spiritual awakening and revival gets underway, I believe God wants organic house churches, *Safe Houses of Hope and Prayer*, to become legendary for their good deeds. I am so convinced of this part of what God is doing that I have written a separate book on this subject which I would encourage you to read.[22]

*". . . the New Testament has quite a bit to say about the importance of good deeds as a manifestation of genuine faith."*

## Some Biblical Perspective

It may come as a surprise to you (frankly, it did to me) that the New Testament has quite a bit to say about the importance of good deeds as a manifestation of genuine faith. And that's where we need to start our discussion. The concept of "good deeds" or "good works" occurs some 32 times in the New Testament. Those 32 occurrences are almost equally divided between two Greek phrases (*agathos ergon* and *kalos ergon*), which are so similar in use and meaning as to be interchangeable. The word *agathos*

---

[22]R. Maurice Smith, **The Least of These: The Role of Good Deeds In A Jesus-Shaped Spirituality** (Spokane: Rising River Media, 2011, 2014), available on our website from Amazon.com.

# Good Deeds And Becoming Legendary

suggests something that is intrinsically good, whereas _kalos_ describes that which, in addition to being intrinsically good, is also outwardly attractive, pleasing or useful. Paul

> *"Where there is no fruit, the viability of the tree must be questioned. Jesus did. So must we."*

uses them interchangeably in 1 Timothy 5:10. The combined idea is that the intrinsically good work which God has begun in the life of every true believer finds its outward manifestation in the fruit of apparent and useful good deeds. And when the visible, useful fruit of good deeds is absent from the life of a professing believer, that absence calls into question whether or not God has actually begun any intrinsically good work in his or her life. Good trees produce good fruit. That's the biblical principle (Matthew 3:10; 7:17-19; 12:33). Where there is no fruit, the viability of the tree must be questioned. Jesus did. So must we.

## Our Works Are Our Witness

*"But the witness which I have is greater than that of John; for the works which the Father has given Me to accomplish, the very works that I do, bear witness of Me, that the Father has sent Me."* (John 5:36)

The most appropriate place to begin our understanding of good works is with Jesus Himself. Jesus was constantly being confronted with the same question by the unbelieving religious leadership of His day: *"How do we know that you are who and what you say you are?"* (See John 2:18; 6:30) On this particular occasion in the fifth chapter of John's gospel Jesus offers His skeptics two reasons why they should believe Him. **First,** He argues that they have the witness of John the Baptist, whom the people and many of the religious leaders regarded as a prophet. But Jesus offers his skeptics a **second**, simple answer to their question: *"Look at my works,"* he says. *"My works speak for themselves."*

This is a bold statement, so bold that it would be easy to conclude that Jesus is establishing some new principle here. But the reality is that He is simply restating an existing truth

> *". . . our works bear witness that God is our Father and that Jesus is our Lord."*

which Jesus taught throughout His ministry: we are known by our fruit. We can state this principle in the same terms that Jesus did here by saying, *"Your works are your witness."* Just as the works of Jesus bore witness to the reality that He came from God, so, too, our works bear witness that God is our Father and that Jesus is our Lord. As we will soon see, just as the Father gave Jesus works to accomplish, so God has appointed good works for every believer to walk in. And our willingness to walk in those good deeds will bear public witness to the private reality of our relationship with Him.

## Are You A Light?

*"You are the light of the world. A city set on a hill cannot be hidden. Nor do men light a lamp, and put it under the peck-measure, but on the lampstand; and it gives light to all who are in the house. Let your light shine before men in such a*

# Good Deeds And Becoming Legendary

*way that they may see your good works (<u>kalos</u> <u>ergon</u>), and glorify your Father who is in heaven."* (Matthew 5:14-16)

Ask yourself a simple question: *"What does it mean for me to be 'the light of the world'?"* An insightful author once asked a challenging question, *"If a can opener won't open any cans, is it really a can opener?"* Just because a certain tool is called a can opener and just because it happens to look like other can openers we have known or used, is it still a can opener if it won't open any cans? Let's apply this to Jesus' parable. . . and to our lives. When is a lamp no longer a lamp? When it no longer does what lamps are suppose to do, namely, give light. Jesus says that you and I (i.e., believers) are the light of the world. He doesn't say that you and I *could* be the light of the world or *should* be the light of the world or *will* be the light of the world. No. He says that you and I *ARE* the light of the world. And what does light do? It shines and *"gives light to all who are in the house."* At this point the natural question for you and me should be, *"How do we do this? How do we let our light shine before men?"*

> *"When is a lamp no longer a lamp? When it no longer does what lamps are suppose to do, namely, give light."*

Fortunately, to prevent us from guessing, Jesus gives us the answer: Through our good deeds. Simply stated, our good deeds are the vehicle through which the light of our Jesus-shaped spirituality shines before men in such a way that they see our good deeds and glorify God as a result. And the Greek word for men here is <u>anthropos</u>, the Greek word for men in general (i.e., unbelievers). Let's be clear on this point, as there seems to be much confusion in the Church on this point. Our good deeds make us a light to an unbelieving world.

In a curious historical note, the early Church historian Eusebius states that story of Jesus' life, death, resurrection and ascension - His life story including His

> *"Our good deeds make us a light to an unbelieving world."*

good deeds - were communicated by Pontius Pilate to the Roman Emperor Tiberius who further presented the report to the Roman Senate.[23] Perhaps this is why Paul could say to King Festus in Acts 26:25-26, *"I am not out of my mind, most excellent Festus, but I utter words of sober truth. For the king knows about these matters, and I speak to him also with confidence, since I am persuaded that none of these things escape his notice; for this has not been done in a corner."* In other words (Maurice's interpretation) Jesus' life and good deeds had become legendary. The light of His life, including His good deeds, had shown in the darkness, not only throughout Palestine but all the way to Rome and its leaders.

Finally, have you ever wondered how Jesus' teaching on this issue affected His own disciples? I think Jesus' words here in Matthew 5 had a profound impact on at least one of His disciples: Simon Peter. Why? Because Peter refers to them years later in 1 Peter: *"Beloved, I urge you as aliens and strangers to abstain from fleshly lusts, which wage war*

---

[23]See Eusebius' *"Church History,"* Book 2, Section 2. Eusebius quotes the Christian Apologist Tertullian who relates this story in full.

# Good Deeds And Becoming Legendary

*against the soul. Keep your behavior excellent among the Gentiles, so that in the thing in which they slander you as evildoers, they may on account of your **good deeds**, as they observe them, glorify God in the day of visitation."* (1 Peter 2:11-12). Did you catch it there at the end of verse 12? Peter tells his readers that, through their excellent behavior among the Gentiles, unbelievers will see their good deeds and will glorify God. Peter got the point. Do we?

## Legendary House Churches

In this coming move of God's Spirit in revival and spiritual awakening, I believe God wants His new wineskins of organic house churches to become legendary once again, particularly in terms of serving others.

***Reflection Question #1 -*** Reflecting on this Chapter, what did you learn about good deeds that you did not know before?

***Reflection Question #2 -*** Take a look at the "Think List" on the following page. Begin brain storming and making a list of potential people, situations and good deeds that could offer an opportunity for you and your house church to show the love of God to someone in need.

# Safe Houses of Hope And Prayer

| Your House Church Think List For "Good Deeds" | |
|---|---|
| *Name of Person* | *What You Can Do* |
| | |
| | |
| | |
| | |
| | |
| | |
| | |
| | |
| | |
| | |
| | |
| | |
| | |
| | |
| | |
| | |

# Chapter 12

## Who Do I Make My Check Out To - Part 1?

Someone once observed that many people never enter into the fullness of Christ because they want to become a Levite for a shirt and ten shekels.[24] The reference is from a sordid episode in the book of Judges (I'll let you read it for yourself, starting in Judges 17:6). In terms of our discussion in this book, such people haven't detoxed or died to self. They are walking in a religion-shaped spirituality, still trying to negotiate the terms of their service. People walking in a religion-shaped spirituality are willing to serve, but only upon a promise of *"a shirt and ten shekels,"* and then only until someone comes along and makes a better offer. A religion-shaped spirituality is easily bought, the only real negotiating point being the sale-price.

I believe there are several critical issues facing the organic house church movement, including such things as defining and restoring what is church (i.e., is it primarily organizational or organic), and re-discovering genuine

> *"Many people never enter into the fullness of Christ because they want to become a Levite for a shirt and ten shekels."*

---

[24]From one of the most influential sermons of recent times, delivered by Pastor Paris Reidhead (date unknown) and available on-line at  http://media.sermonindex.net/0/SID0290.mp3

# Safe Houses of Hope And Prayer

biblical community and how Christians can work and network together (which is what *Safe Houses of Hope and Prayer* is all about). But what may turn out to be one of the defining and determining issues for the future of the organic house church movement could be how organic house churches understand and handle the issue of money and giving. And that is the topic for the rest of this Chapter. Consider yourself warned!

## The Challenge of Giving

The comedian Henny Youngman once quipped, *"I've got all the money I'll ever need . . . If I die by 4 o'clock."* I think he would have felt right at home in the house church movement. In fact, I think I've finally figured out why there are so many "prosperity gospel" preachers and teachers today. The answer is really quite simple when you think about it: It pays better (Well, duh!). At least in this life. Unfortunately, the accounting that really matters comes later, after it's too late to do anything about it. Now, don't worry. I'm not planning to begin preaching prosperity and wealth. I'm allergic to polyester and hair spray, and despite repeated attempts, I still can't stretch the word "God" into three syllables.

Not too long ago the pastor of a local seeker-friendly megachurch related the following statistics regarding Christian giving:

*Giving Statistic #1 -* 80% of all giving in the church is done by 20% of attendees.

*Giving Statistic #2 -* The remaining 20% of all money is

given by the next 30% of attendees.

***Giving Statistic #3 -*** If you're following the math, this means that 100% of all giving is done by 50% of church attendees.

***Giving Statistic #4 -*** The remaining 50% of church attendees give . . . ***nothing!*** Ouch!

So, it should come as no surprise that according to The Barna Group in a study of giving for 2012, only 5% of adult Americans and only 12% of born again adults tithed (gave 10% of their income).[25] And

*"Christian giving as a percentage of income has been in a prolonged decline for over 40 years."*

Christian giving as a percentage of income has been in a prolonged decline for over 40 years. According to statistics provided by Empty Tomb, Inc., in 1968 the average percentage of one's income given to the Church was 3.1%, but by 2011 that percentage had fallen to 2.3%, a decline of 25%.[26]

## Giving From a Religion-Shaped Spirituality

Most financial giving in traditional, institutional church is the

[25]See *"American Donor Trends,"* April 12, 2013, The Barna Group, posted online at https://www.barna.org.

[26]John L. Ronsvalle and Sylvia Ronsvalle, *"The State of Church Giving Through 2011,"* Twenty-Third Edition 2013, (Champaign, Illinois: empty tomb, inc., 2013). Available in book format from Amazon.com

out-flow of a religion-shaped spirituality which builds its behavior around the answers to two basic financial questions:

***Financial Question #1: What does God require?*** This question applies specifically to the responsibility of the believer when it comes to giving. It's a question in search of the minimum required contribution which, if met, will please God and prove that we are good stewards of our money. The standard answer is that *"God will really bless you if you 'tithe'"* (give 10%). There are three basic

> *"We don't get to pick and choose the 'Law of Tithing' as binding on believers today just because the building fund is behind on its fund raising goals."*

problems with this answer. ***First,*** under the law, the full Old Testament tithe was not 10%. When all of the required tithes, double tithes and special tithes were included, the damage was closer to 33%. Ouch! ***Second,*** tithing is not taught anywhere in the New Testament (read that sentence again). ***Third,*** if the Old Testament law of the tithe is binding upon New Testament believers, then so are all 612 requirements of the Law. We don't get to pick and choose the Law of Tithing as binding on believers today just because the building fund is behind on its fund raising goals.

***Financial Question #2: Is he (or she) worth "a shirt and ten shekels."*** This is where life in the church can get really ugly, as Christians argue over who is worth what. All too often the values expressed resemble Donald Trump's

# Who Do I Make My Check Out To - Part 1?

infamous board room more than they do God's Throne Room. The questions asked seem to be more pertinent to *"Who can 'earn their keep' and run the organization and its activities"* than they are to *"Who is God raising up to equip His Church and facilitate His harvest, and what do they need in terms of resources to do this?"*

## Giving From A Jesus-Shaped Spirituality

If the organic house church movement, walking in a Jesus-shaped spirituality, is to grow and prosper and have a generational impact for the Kingdom of God, we must begin offering different answers to these fundamental questions regarding money and finances in the Church.

*Financial Question #1: What does God require?* Here's the biblical answer: Nothing! That's right, I said nothing (you might want to read that again, since you may be recovering from shock and apoplexy at this moment). Nowhere in the New Testament does God require tithing or any other

> *"Nowhere in the New Testament does God require tithing or any other form of compulsory giving."*

form of compulsory giving (parables on stewardship not withstanding). This is what Paul tells the believers in Corinth in 2 Corinthians 9:7, *"Let each one do just as he has purposed in his heart; **not** grudgingly or **under compulsion**; for God loves a cheerful giver."* The square peg of a religion-shaped spirituality can stare at this verse all day and not understand that the New Testament has given God's people a new standard: uncoerced, cheerful giving. More about this later.

**Financial Question #2: Is he (or she) worth "a shirt and ten shekels."** O.K., from the perspective of a Jesus-shaped spirituality the answer is *"No! So stop asking!"* That's right. A Jesus-shaped spirituality rejects the entire question as irrelevant. We need to ask a whole new question: *"Who are the gifted and mature 5-fold people whom God is raising up to equip His Church for the harvest; and what resources do they need from us to move their ministry forward?"*

### The Unresolved Tension

There is an unresolved tension within the organic house church movement today regarding money, giving and finances. Having come out of the religion-shaped spirituality of institutional Christianity and its *"a shirt and ten shekels"* approach to ministry, many

> *". . . many organic house church practitioners have rejected the notion of anyone being compensated or paid to do ministry."*

organic house church practitioners have rejected the notion of anyone being compensated or paid to do ministry. Their view is that everyone in ministry should make tents (i.e., have a paying day job) and do ministry on the side, like Paul supposedly did in the New Testament. This approach (I believe) is having a profound negative impact on the organic house church movement. For example, I have met and talked with several gifted institutional church pastors who want to

# Who Do I Make My Check Out To - Part 1?

leave their traditional churches and pursue organic house church except for the financial reality of not knowing how they would provide for themselves and their families. I believe this *"let them make tents"* approach to money and ministry is misguided for the following reasons:

**1. The example of Jesus and the Disciples.** This approach contradicts the clear example of Jesus and His disciples. Consider the following passage:

*"Soon afterward he went on through cities and villages, proclaiming and bringing the good news of the kingdom of God. And the twelve were with him, and also some women who had been healed of evil spirits and infirmities: Mary, called Magdalene, from whom seven demons had gone out, and Joanna, the wife of Chuza, Herod's household manager, and Susanna, <u>and many others, who provided for them out of their means</u>."* (Luke 8:1-3)

Jesus didn't do carpentry at night to support His ministry work, and the disciples had left their jobs to follow Jesus. Both Jesus and His disciples were supported financially by the gifts of many people. In addition, when Jesus sent out the seventy-two in Luke 10, he specifically instructed them to live by the support of those to whom they ministered, *"And remain in the same house, eating and drinking what they provide, for <u>the laborer deserves his wages</u>."* (Luke 10:7). Why should that be any

> *". . . when Jesus sent out the seventy-two in Luke 10, he specifically instructed them to live by the support of those to whom they ministered."*

different today?

**2. The misunderstood example of Paul.** Some people want to argue that the Apostle Paul supported his ministry by holding down a secular job (i.e., making tents, see Acts 18:1-3). But this is only partially true. In 1 Corinthians 9 Paul defends his ministry by arguing that he and other workers **had a right** to expect support from the churches they worked with, but that he had not exercised that right in order to avoid hindering the gospel.

*"If we have sown spiritual things among you, is it too much if we reap material things from you? If others share this rightful claim on you, do not we even more? Nevertheless, we have not made use of this right, but we endure anything rather than put an obstacle in the way of the gospel of Christ."* (1 Corinthians 9:11-12)

The only time Paul made tents (held an outside job) was when the churches he was working with were too spiritually immature to understand and fulfill their responsibilities to support Paul's work! Paul summarizes his understanding concerning paid ministry as follows:

*"Do you not know that those who are employed in the temple service get their food from the temple, and those who serve at the altar share in the sacrificial offerings? In the same way,* **the Lord commanded** *that those who proclaim the gospel should get their living by the gospel."* (1 Corinthians 9:13-14)

**Question:** Precisely when and where did the Lord Jesus give such a command? **Answer:** In Luke 10:7 when he sent out the seventy-two. To state this another way, a spiritually mature house church will understand and embrace this principle of supporting those gifted and mature individuals in their midst who devote themselves to equipping the Church.

**3. The clear teaching of Scripture.** We have already seen that Jesus Himself taught His disciples the principle of being supported by those to whom they minister (again, see Luke 10). In addition, the Apostle Paul repeats this principle in his instructions to his young pastor-disciple Timothy,

*"Let the elders who rule well be considered worthy of double honor, especially those who labor in preaching and teaching. For the Scripture says, 'You shall not muzzle an ox when it treads out the grain,' and, 'The laborer deserves his wages.'"* (1 Timothy 5:17-18)

According to Paul, quoting first from the Old Testament Scriptures(Deuteronomy 25:4) and then from the words of Jesus Himself (Luke 10:7), the laborer who devotes himself (or herself) to the work of the ministry is *"worthy of his wages."*

## Radical Sacrificial Giving

When it comes to money and ministry, I believe Scripture maintains what I describe as a radical balance between *"radical sacrificial giving"* on the one hand and *"radical sacrificial living"* on the other. I this section I want to look at what the New Testament has to say about *"radical sacrificial giving."* We'll save the *"radical sacrificial living"* for the next chapter.

# Safe Houses of Hope And Prayer

The heart of a Jesus-shaped spirituality is the biblical principle of spiritual transformation. The Kingdom of God transforms everything it touches. It transforms religious square pegs into spiritual round pegs which can fit into the spiritual round holes of the

> *". . . the biblical standard for giving has been transformed from 'tithing out of obligation' to 'radical sacrificial giving' out of a transformed life."*

new thing God is doing. This transformation includes how we view money, and in the Church it transforms both the questions we ask and the answers we give. As part of that transformation, I believe the biblical standard for giving has been transformed from *"tithing out of obligation"* to *"radical sacrificial giving"* out of a transformed life.

Simply put, if your finances have been touched by the Kingdom of God, your understanding of them will be transformed. As we saw earlier in Chapter 5 ("Life Is Messy!"), the New Testament transforms and redefines the believer's responsibilities before God in nearly every area of life. What does this have to do with money and giving in the New Testament? Simply this. The New Testament transforms the believer's responsibility concerning money and giving from an outward fixed percentage to an inward attitude of *radical sacrificial giving*. There are no New Testament commands or examples of believers tithing.[27] But the Scriptures offer us   numerous examples of *radical*

---

[27]The word "tithe" occurs only 5 times in the New Testament, none with reference to the Christian's responsibility to give.

# Who Do I Make My Check Out To - Part 1?

*sacrificial giving.* Consider the following:

**1. God Himself -** That's right. Radical sacrificial giving begins at the top. God Himself is our example, and God doesn't tithe. Instead, He gives radically and sacrificially. God gave to us radically and sacrificially by giving to us unworthy sinners the unfathomable gift of His Son. God Himself spared no expense to redeem us from our fallen and lost condition. And so Paul could declare, at the end of

> *"God Himself is our example, and God doesn't tithe. Instead, He gives radically and sacrificially."*

his discourse on radical sacrificial giving in 2 Corinthians 8-9, *"Thanks be to God for His indescribable gift!"* (2 Corinthians 9:15). A Jesus-shaped spirituality understands that it really is impossible to out-give God! *"He who did not spare His own Son, but delivered Him up for us all, how will He not also with Him freely give us all things?"* (Romans 832) Amen! God is a radical sacrificial giver!

**2. The Widow -** In Mark 12:41ff the author paints a fascinating picture. He tells us that Jesus *"sat down opposite the treasury, and began observing how the multitude were putting money into the treasury."* Imagine this scene. Jesus, God in human form, sitting there at the Temple Treasury, studying people's giving habits! He sat there watching as *"many rich people were putting in large sums."* You would think that Jesus would be impressed with that kind of generosity. But He wasn't (remember, you can't out give God, so it is hard to impress Him!). But then someone caught

Jesus' attention. A widow. A poor widow we are told. She put in two small copper coins. What were they worth? Around one sixty-fourth (yep, 1/64th) of a *denarius* (a *denarius* was equal to one day's working wage). Her gift was a mere pittance,

> *"Her gift was a mere pittance, compared with the gifts of the rich donors who visited the Treasury that day. But unlike them, her gift was radical and sacrificial."*

compared with the gifts of the rich donors who visited the Treasury that day. But unlike them, her gift was radical and sacrificial. Of all the gifts placed into the Treasury that day, only her's earned Jesus attention and blessing: *"This poor widow put in more than all the contributors to the treasury; for they all put in out of their surplus, but she, out of her poverty (literally, her "destitution"), put in all she owned, all she had to live on."* Had this poor widow tithed her income. Hardly. She had given everything, *"all she had to live on."* And God Himself, sitting there in human flesh, had watched and taken notice.

**3. Zaccheus -** In Luke 19 we learn the story of Zaccheus. He was a publican, a Jew with a public contract with Rome to collect taxes at a profit on their behalf. We all know the story of Zaccheus climbing the tree to get a better view of Jesus and Jesus calling him down, saying, *"Zaccheus, hurry and come down, for today I must stay at your house."* (Luke 19:5) But a curious thing occurs in verse 8. Zaccheus tells Jesus, *"Behold, Lord, half of my possessions I will give to the poor, and if I have defrauded anyone of anything, I will give back four times as much."* Hmm, so much for tithing. Zaccheus wasn't responding to any requirement of the Law concerning either tithing or fraud. Under the Law a thief was required to return what he had stolen plus an additional 20%. But Zaccheus, responding out of a transformed life, promises to repay 400% to anyone he has defrauded, plus to give not 10% but 50% of everything he owns to the poor. There was no such requirement in the Law! This wasn't the response of a religion-shaped spirituality seeking to meet the requirements of the Law. This was the response of a Jesus-shaped spirituality. A response of radical sacrificial giving on the part of someone whose life had been transformed by a powerful personal encounter with Jesus!

**4. Barnabas -** Actually, his name was Joseph, not Barnabas. But he had such a gift of encouraging others that the Apostles had nick-named him Barnabas, which *means "Son of Encouragement."* The young church in Jerusalem had some profound needs as a result of a large and quick harvest of new believers. Thousands of people had come to new-found faith in Christ as a result of Pentecost and subsequent events. Many of them had stayed in town to learn more about their new faith and the Church was now confronted with the challenge of how to meet these overwhelming needs. Barnabas saw the need and responded. We are told that Barnabas *"owned a tract of land, sold it and brought the money and laid it at the apostles feet"* (Acts 4:37). This wasn't the response of a religion-shaped spirituality and its obligation to tithe. This was the response of a Jesus-shaped spirituality and its call to radical sacrificial giving to meet the needs of the Kingdom.

**5. The Macedonians -** Like the story of the widow we saw in Mark 12:41, this example is both heart breaking and convicting. Writing to the young believers in Corinth who were still wrestling with the whole issue giving, Paul tells the Corinthian believers about the believers in Macedonia who had recently given into his ministry,

*"We want you to know, brothers, about the grace of God that has been given among the churches of Macedonia, for in a severe test of affliction, their abundance of joy and their extreme poverty have overflowed in a wealth of generosity on their part. For they gave according to their means, as I can testify, and beyond their means, of their own accord, begging us earnestly for the favor of taking part in the relief of the saints — and this, not as we expected, but they gave themselves first to the Lord and then by the will of God to us."* (2 Corinthians 8:1-5)

I could spend a whole chapter here explaining this passage and not do it justice. The language of the Greek alone is overpowering as Paul describes people who, as we used to say back home in North Carolina, were "dirt poor."[28] Yet, in

> *"Yet, in the midst of their 'deep poverty' they overflowed both with joy and with liberal giving."*

the midst of their deep poverty they overflowed both with joy and with liberal giving. According to Paul, the Macedonian believers didn't simply give *"according to their ability"* (i.e., *"I've got it, so I'll give it"*), but *"beyond their ability."* This isn't the religion-shaped spirituality of obligation and tithing. This

---

[28]Back home, a "dirt poor" family referred to a house that only had a dirt floor. As a boy I had friends who lived is such houses.

# Who Do I Make My Check Out To - Part 1?

is the Jesus-shaped spirituality of joyful, radical sacrificial giving by people like the poor widow of Mark 12:41, people who had nothing and gave everything . . . and then gave some more.

## So, Where Do We Go From Here?

*Reflection Question #1 -* How has this Chapter challenged your understanding of money and giving?

*Reflection Question #2 -* How would you define *"radical sacrificial giving"*? What could that look like in your own life?

*Reflection Question #3 -* Like Jesus sitting beside the Temple Treasury, if God were to study and take notice of your giving habits today, what would He notice about you (or about me) and how would He respond?

# Safe Houses of Hope And Prayer

# Chapter 13

## Who Do I Make My Check Out To - Part 2

*"Many of us Christians have become extremely skillful in arranging our lives so as to admit the truth of Christianity without being embarrassed by its implications. We arrange things so that we can get on well enough without Divine aid, while at the same time ostensibly seeking it. We boast in the Lord but watch carefully that we never get caught depending on Him . . . . Pseudo faith always arranges a way out to serve in case God fails it. Real faith knows only one way and gladly allows itself to be stripped of any second way or makeshift substitutes. For true faith, it is either God or total collapse."*[29]

### Radical Sacrificial Living

In the previous section we talked about the need for a Jesus-shaped spirituality which manifests itself in *radical sacrificial giving*. Now, we need to flip the coin and talk about the need for a Jesus-shaped spirituality which manifests itself in *radical sacrificial living*. We are in desperate need of a generation of Christians, walking in a Jesus-shaped spirituality, whose lives have been set on fire by the Spirit of God, who are willing to trust God without reservation and who are divinely compelled for both radical kingdom giving . . . and radical sacrificial living.

---

[29]A.W. Tozer, *The Root of the Righteous* (Camp Hill, PA: WingSpread Publishers, 2007).

# Safe Houses of Hope And Prayer

I am not in a place to tell you what radical sacrificial giving, or radical sacrificial living, should mean or look like in your life or in the life of your house church. That's between you and God. What I am certain of is that the Church is entering one of the most challenging seasons of ministry in its recent history. The spiritual battle for our generation is raging. And God is about to release great blessing for those who are willing to serve Him radically in the Kingdom for the next several years. And He is going to hold each of us accountable for how we utilize the resources he has given us to advance His Kingdom causes during this season.

## A Personal Journey

My wife and I met while on staff with Campus Crusade for Christ in the late 70s. There we learned what it meant to raise monthly financial support and to live by faith (to be brutally honest, we hated it!). Later when I attended seminary, we did the same thing. We lived by faith, raised support through an organization called Student Ministries, worked on a church staff as a paid youth director, and worked part time to support our school and ministry activities. Upon graduation we decided that we had experienced all of the living by faith that we wanted. I decided to go into business, to make money and give to ministries. Unfortunately, my plan wasn't God's plan. We spent the next 15 years or so going bankrupt. As we picked up the pieces and prayed about what to do next, we came to the realization that God had always been calling us to *radical sacrificial living* (as opposed to giving). Now, as we answered His call into house church ministry, we prayerfully concluded that God was again calling us to live by faith, trusting God to meet our needs and living on whatever He provided.

As two people who have experienced financial failure, including foreclosure, bankruptcy and other financial disasters that other Christians only have nightmares about, I

> *"He is no fool who gives what he cannot keep, to gain what he cannot lose."*

suspect my wife and I have a unique perspective on these things. Having literally suffered the loss of all things, my wife and I have made a personal commitment to live by faith and to never allow money to deter us from pursuing God's Kingdom purposes for our lives. We refuse to allow our lives and our ministry to be ruled by the pursuit of *"a shirt and ten shekels."* As a result we have come to understand what Jim Elliott meant when he said, *"He is no fool who gives what he cannot keep, to gain what he cannot lose."* That, in a nutshell, is *radical sacrificial living*, the overflow of a transformed life.

## An Example From History

Our personal story is minor compared to many others. There are shining examples of radical sacrificial giving throughout church history. One of my favorites comes from the life of John Wesley, whom we have already talked about in this book. During the Evangelical Awakening in England during the mid-1700s John Wesley offered himself as a living example of a lifestyle dedicated to radical sacrificial giving and free from the love of money.

# Safe Houses of Hope And Prayer

At the beginning of each year Wesley calculated what he would need to live on for the coming year. Once that figure was calculated he made a conscious choice to give away everything in excess of that modest amount. In one particular year Wesley lived on approximately £30 (in today's currency, approximately $2,400). But in that same year he earned and gave away an additional £1,400, which means that he gave away nearly 98% of his earnings for that year. Early in his long ministry, in 1743, Wesley wrote, *"If I leave behind me £10 . . . you and all mankind bear witness against me that I lived and died a thief and a robber."* Wesley regarded both his life and his wealth as a stewardship, entrusted to him by God for the benefit of those around him.

Wesley believed in industry and hard work, helping many fellow Methodists to start successful businesses. His personal financial philosophy was

> *"Gain all you can, save all you can, give all you can."* - John Wesley

simple and he expressed it regularly in a simple motto: *"Gain all you can, save all you can, give all you can."* As his popularity and notoriety grew throughout England, the sale of his books and pamphlets could have made Wesley a wealthy man. Instead he chose to pursue a life of *radical sacrificial giving* on the one hand and *radical sacrificial living* on the other.

In the year 1776 Wesley received a note from the Commissioner of Excise. At that time the British Government imposed a luxury excise tax upon all silver plate (dinnerware, etc.). The Commissioner of Excise claimed that Wesley owned more silver plate than he had declared and paid tax

# Who Do I Make My Check Out To - Part 2?

on. Wesley responded curtly but profoundly, *"I have two silver spoons at London and two at Bristol. This is all the plate I have at present, and I shall not buy any more while so many round me want bread."* Is it any wonder that Wesley never heard back from The Commissioner of Excise? It's hard to argue with the eloquence of a Jesus-shaped spirituality.

But Wesley did more. Concerned about debt among the poor, he created the forerunner what today would be called credit unions. The *"Benevolent Loan Fund"* made short-term loans to Methodists in financial need. Wesley personally solicited capital donations for the fund, and loaned money on more than one occasion to assist a Methodist to start a business. In addition, Wesley founded the *"Strangers Society"* which, according to Wesley, was *"instituted wholly for the relief not of our Society, but of poor, sick, friendless strangers."* These early credit unions were intended to assist individuals in need who might have no other alternative.

On the eve of his death with his strength failing, John Wesley closed his personal financial account book with these words:

*"For upwards of 86 years I have kept my accounts exactly, I will not attempt it any longer, being satisfied with the continual conviction that I save all I can, and give all I can - that is all I have."*

Such self-imposed poverty has its consequences. It was said of John Wesley that when he died he left behind only three things: a well-worn clerical robe, an extensive personal library, and the Methodist Church. When the day arrives for us to settle and close our accounts here on earth in

# Safe Houses of Hope And Prayer

preparation for the reckoning of heaven, may the same be said of us.

## So, Where Do We Go From Here?

I want to talk now about how all of this relates to organic house church.

*First,* I want to re-iterate that the New Testament teaches *radical sacrificial giving* on the one hand, and *radical sacrificial living* on the other. *Radical sacrificial giving* means that believers are no longer under an obligation to give a certain amount or a fixed percentage of their income to God. Rather, God calls all believers to give abundantly and cheerfully - even radically - to the work of the Kingdom and to support those mature and gifted five-fold leaders who devote themselves full time to equipping the Church for the harvest. *Radical sacrificial living* means that those whom God has gifted and called to devote themselves to equipping the Church for the work of ministry trust Him to fully meet their needs while refusing to sell themselves for the offer of *"a shirt and ten shekels."*

*Second,* although organic house churches do not have the financial burden of supporting buildings, programs and staff, this does *not* mean that organic house churches are off the hook when it comes to their biblical responsibilities regarding stewardship, money and giving. Each believer and each house church must ask (and answer) the question, *"What does God's call to radical sacrificial giving mean for me and for us, and how do we turn that into practical financial support?"* Are there benevolence needs within the body which should be met? What about needs among people we are trying to reach out to? What about outreach giving *to "the least of these"*? Are there five-fold people ministering in our midst full time who need support? Are there apostolic house church planters we should be supporting?

*Reflection Question #1 -* How has this Chapter challenged you concerning your understanding of money and giving?

*Reflection Question #2 -* The average Christian gives around 2.3% of their income to the Church. How do you plan to change that situation in your own life?

*Reflection Question #3 -* How would the Holy Spirit have you change your giving in order to 1) minister to people in need and to *"the least of these,"* and 2) support people in your midst, house church planters and others who are equipping the Church?

# Safe Houses of Hope And Prayer

# Chapter 14

## Teaching, Preaching and Talking

I hope this doesn't come as a surprise to anyone, but most evangelical churches in America are NOT led by pastors, although that may be the title on the office door. They are led by teachers. The mantra of the typical pastor search committee in a typical evangelical church is *"We need to find someone who is a good Bible teacher."* As a result of this *"teacher-philos,"* budding evangelical leaders from Bible schools and seminaries across America come to regard teaching as the gift that gets you noticed and promoted. You can make a name for yourself and build a following by showing off how well you can speak and teach.

These are the people to whom traditional evangelicalism affords rock star status. Even our church architecture perpetuates this story of rock star status. Megachurch auditoriums with theater or stadium style seating, all focused upon a center-stage, complete with

> *"In the Kingdom of God, discipleship never takes place on stages or under the glare of spotlights."*

spotlights, to focus all attention upon the "rock star" teacher/preacher who is about to take the stage and perform. And perform they do, week after week, entertaining the assembled multitudes, blissfully unaware that - in spite of their rock star popularity, including sales of their books and DVDs in the foyer - they are raising up a generation of spiritual mules who will never be able to reproduce what they are hearing and watching.

In the Kingdom of God, discipleship never takes place on stages or under the glare of spotlights. While there may be numerous megachurch teachers and preachers who can successfully lay claim to having preached to more people than Jesus ever did, the stark reality that they have personally discipled fewer men who have had less of an impact for the Kingdom of God makes their claim shallow at best. The goal of organic church is not size or numbers, but impact.

> *"The goal of organic church is not size or numbers, but impact."*

## A Different Model of Organic Teaching

Here's my advice. Lose the stage. Lose the spotlight. Let go of the religious square peg of how this has been done in the past. We need a different model of teaching in organic house church. We need a biblical model of teaching that offers people a Jesus-shaped spirituality, a spiritual round peg that can easily and quickly adapt to the changing environment of a spiritual awakening.

The best way to illustrate this need is to tell a story from the Great Welsh Revival of 1904. This revival came to be known as *"the singing revival"* because of the tremendous amount of worshipful singing that occurred in many of the meetings. Nearly every church in Wales was filled to capacity 7 nights a week for 18 months, and over 5% of the population of the

# Teaching, Preaching and Talking

nation professed Christ for the first time and joined a Church! But the revival was frequently criticized for a lack of Bible teaching and preaching.

A well respected London Journalist and Christian named William Thomas Stead traveled to Wales to personally witness the revival. His articles, which appeared in several Christian publications, popularized the revival among Stead's British readers in London. He was asked specifically about the lack of teaching and preaching in many of the services. Here is W. T. Stead's observation as it appeared in *The Methodist Times* for December 15, 1904:

*"Do you think that teaching is what people want in a revival? These people, all the people in a land like ours, are taught to death, preached to insensibility. They all know the essential truths. They know that they are not living as they ought to live, and no amount of teaching will add anything to that conviction.*

*To hear some people talk you would imagine that the best way to get a sluggard out of bed is to send a tract on astronomy showing him that according to the fixed and eternal law the sun will rise at a certain hour in the morning. The sluggard does not deny it. He is entirely convinced of it. But what he knows is that it is precious cold at sunrise on a winter's morning, and it is very snug and warm between the blankets. What the sluggard needs is to be well shaken, and in case of need to be pulled out of bed. 'Roused,' the Revival calls it. And the Revival is a rouser rather than a teacher. And that is why I think those Churches which want to go on dozing in the ancient ways had better hold a special series of prayer meetings that the Revival may be prevented coming their way."*

This story serves to make several points. ***First,*** one hundred years after those words were written, most Christians today are sluggards in need of rousing as opposed to students in need of more teaching. What we need today is a burning coal fresh from God's altar (Isaiah 6:6), rather than a fresh PowerPoint presentation fresh-off the Pastor's laptop.

***Second,*** when things are quiet in the life of the Church, teachers tend to fill the void of divine silence with teaching, giving answers to questions which no one in particular is asking. But when the Spirit of God begins to move in power during times of spiritual awakening - like the times described by W. T. Stead - newly awakened people begin asking a whole new set of questions based upon their recent experiences. At this point, the revival becomes both a rouser and a teacher. One appeals to the head, while the other appeals to the heart.

*". . . most Christians today are sluggards in need of 'rousing' as opposed to students in need of more 'teaching'."*

In terms of educational learning theory, it's the difference between *cognitive* learning and *affective* learning. *Cognitive* learning appeals to the head by imparting information and facts. *Affective* learning satisfies the heart by

*"Once the heart has been 'roused,' the head is much more willing to be taught."*

engaging our emotions in a way that leads to changed behavior. Once the heart has been roused, the head is much more willing to be taught. This, I believe, was W. T. Stead's point, a point we need to embrace today.

## Don't Answer Questions No One Is Asking

An answer without a question is a truth destined for oblivion in someone's notebook somewhere. But an answer to a question arising from a life experience will last in our memory for a lifetime. Do you even remember what the pastor of your church preached or taught on six months ago? What three life changing truths did you learn from his sermon six weeks ago? Can't remember? Then how important was it, really?

Now, do you remember the last time you saw someone delivered from demonic oppression? You can probably remember most, if not all, of the details! I certainly can, and so can Jaime. And that deserves a story.

Jaime is a young woman my wife and I have worked with for several years. Part of her spiritual journey into the Kingdom of God involved a prolonged deliverance from satanism and the demonic. Her struggle with the demonic was intense, even following her conversion. But all along the way I purposely did not force answers on her. Instead, knowing how these things tend to manifest in growing crises, I chose to wait for her to ask the question.

It is my experience that we Christians have a tendency to give unsolicited answers before people have either the opportunity or the need to ask the question (need as determined by them, not by us). Then we wonder why people don't listen to our brilliant teaching. *Answer:* Because we spend most of our time talking to ourselves, rather than listening for the question. This is what Scripture means when it

*"We Christians have a tendency to give unsolicited answers before people have either the opportunity or the need to ask the question."*

warns us against casting our pearls before swine (Matthew 7:6). To not cast pearls before swine means don't give something valuable (like "pearls" of biblical truth) to people who cannot appreciate it. It does no good to give a spiritually blind man glasses, or more truth to stare at. Chances are they will trample it under foot and attack you in the process.

For Jaime, the need and the question came soon enough. As I knew it would, the demonic harassment reached a point where she could no longer fight it alone. *"Please help me,"* she asked over the phone. My wife and I quickly arranged to meet with Jaime and her mom, bringing along several prophetically gifted people from our house church network who had experience dealing with the demonic. Before we went, while I was praying about what we should do and how we should proceed, the Lord led me to the following passage:

*"When the unclean spirit has gone out of a person, it passes through waterless places seeking rest, and finding none it says, 'I will return to my house from which I came.' And when it comes, it finds the house swept and put in order. Then it goes and brings seven other spirits more evil than itself, and they enter and dwell there. And the last state of that person*

## Teaching, Preaching and Talking

*is worse than the first."* (Luke 11: 24-26)

I sensed the Lord saying, *"It's time for Jaime to take a stand."* When we met with her and her mom I asked her to describe what was going on. She informed me that a single demon had been harassing her, but now there were eight of them (she has the unusual ability to see these things). I said, *"Jaime, you've had a very biblical experience."* I then read this passage from Luke and asked her, *"How many demons were there in this passage? And how many demons have been harassing you?"* We quickly did the math, *"One plus seven of his friends; that's eight! The same number as in this passage!"*

The expression on her face at that moment was priceless, declaring to me that she got it! Next, I turned to Ephesians Chapter 6:10-17 and explained the biblical importance of "standing firm" against the devil. I walked her through a re-commitment of her life to Christ as a declaration to the demonic realm regarding her commitment to "stand firm" in Christ, and we ended the night by taking communion and praying together.

For Jaime, her life-crisis became a powerful teachable moment. The demonic encounter had roused her heart (that's *affective*) and generated a question which the truth of God's word directly addressed (that's *cognitive*). For me, teaching became easy in that moment as the *cognitive* truth of God's word found a roused and willing heart and spoke directly to the *affective* need of Jaime's life and emotions.

As we saw earlier in Chapter 6, the spiritual life of our house churches should include formal *cognitive* teaching (*didache* -

a formal body of truth or doctrine). There are times when formal teaching is important and needed. But the further removed any cognitive teaching is from the *affective* learning which arises from the life experiences of people in our house churches, the more we will be offering answers to questions which people simply aren't asking (the whole "pearls and swine" thing). Cognitive learning and head knowledge alone will lead to pride (1 Corinthians 8:1) and will be devoid of practical application or changed lives. Affective, experiential learning alone will eventually devolve into mysticism, sentimentality, error and experiences contrary to truth.

Remember that formal cognitive teaching alone (the kind of teaching most Christians are familiar with) is not the secret ingredient to a successful house church. God wants His people to experience the entire body in all its various parts and gifts functioning together as we worship together as a community. This happens through one person bringing a teaching, another person bringing a song, another praying for healing for others in the group, another exercising a gift of intercession to pray over those in need, and another bringing a prophetic word. All of these things working together will result in both cognitive and affective learning with the result that lives will be changed and the saints will be equipped and encouraged for greater service!

> *"God wants His people to experience the entire body in all its various parts and gifts functioning together as we worship together as a community."*

House church leaders should prepared to *"teach on the go,"* utilizing teachable moments that God supernaturally and sovereignly provides to engage in both affective (*"here's the experience"*) and cognitive (*"here's what the experience means"*) learning as God leads. When life is spiritually quiet in the Church, the teaching gift may need to step back while other gifts minister to the body.

## Preach Your Heart Out

I was in my Freshman year of Seminary when it happened. It was my first introduction to the annual Senior's preaching and Bible reading competition. In a nutshell, once every year graduating seminary students competed before a student and faculty panel. There were two categories: preaching and Bible reading (with money as the reward, of course).

When I mentioned the upcoming competition to my Hebrew teacher, himself a graduating senior, he rolled his eyes and quipped, *"Yea, I think they should have more categories. We should have a healing competition, a tongues speaking competition, and a 'raising the dead' competition."* His tongue was firmly in his cheek by this point in the conversation.

In case my point isn't obvious to all, Christians love to preach. We always have. We encourage it. We teach people how to do it in our bible schools and seminaries (it's called *"homiletics"*). We even have competitions to see who is the best at it. And we build our church buildings and facilities so as to provide a platform for this particular style of communication (the whole megachurch stadium seating and stage thing again).

# Safe Houses of Hope And Prayer

The New Testament book of Acts records roughly 15 sermons or messages delivered in a public setting of some type. Given that the book of Acts covers roughly a 32 year period, that would be an average of about one sermon every two years. Not exactly a preaching frenzy.

In the New Testament there are two primary words that are often translated as "preach." The first is the Greek word _euangelidzo_ which is used almost exclusively of proclaiming the good news of the

> "... it isn't at all clear that the early church 'preached to the choir' the way we do in traditional church today."

gospel to those who have not heard it. From this Greek word we get our English word "evangelize." The emphasis is upon proclaiming a message of good news. The second New Testament word for "preach" is the Greek word _kerusso_, which means _"to be a herald."_ It often described an official herald and literally meant to perform the actions of a herald by making an official proclamation.

O.K., while there is no question that the early Church preached or proclaimed the good news of the gospel, it is **not** as clear that these two words were used extensively to describe how the early Church communicated truth in the context of its daily life and teaching. In other words, it isn't at all clear that the early church preached to the choir the way we do in traditional church today.

# Teaching, Preaching and Talking

## Let's Talk About That

This leads us to the third biblical word that was also important in the life of the New Testament Church, a word which seems to receive little attention in most churches today. It is the word *dialegomai*, from which we derive our English word "dialogue."

The word *dialegomai* comes from two Greek words, *dia* (a preposition meaning *"through"*) and *lego* (a verb meaning *"to talk,"* hence, *"to talk through"*). In the every day Greek of the 1$^{st}$ Century, including Jewish writers such as Philo and Josephus, over half of all occurrences of this word had to do with a "conversation." Linguist W.E. Vine suggests that *dialegomai* primarily means,

*"to think different things with oneself, hence, to ponder or to resolve in one's mind, then, to converse; most frequently to reason or dispute with, not by way of a sermon, but by a discourse of a more conversational character."*

In other words, the word *dialegomai* was used to describe a reasoned conversation - a dialogue - with an intent to persuade. For this reason it is often translated "reasoned," as in Acts 19:9,

*"But when some became stubborn and continued in unbelief, speaking evil of the Way before the congregation, he withdrew from them and took the disciples with him, reasoning daily in the hall of Tyrannus."*

When we look at the Book of Acts we discover that the Apostle Paul actually preferred the concept of *dialegomai*.

# Safe Houses of Hope And Prayer

Indeed, the Book of Acts records that a change of emphasis took place during Paul's missionary journeys. Beginning with Paul's first missionary journey (see Acts 13:32) until his ministry in Athens during the second missionary journey the predominant word used to describe Paul's message and ministry was *euangelidzo*, the proclamation of good news, specifically to unbelievers. But *euangelidzo* never occurs after Acts 17:18 and Paul's time in Athens. Instead, the word *dialegomai* becomes the predominant word throughout the remainder of Paul's ministry.[30]

This change of emphasis suggests that Paul came to understand the importance of carrying on a reasoned conversation - a dialogue - both with unbelievers he was seeking to lead to Christian faith, and with believers he was seeking to instruct and encourage in their faith (see Acts 20:7 & 9).

*"Too many Christians today have lost the ability to carry on a genuine conversational dialogue with either believers or unbelievers."*

Too many Christians today have lost the ability to carry on a genuine conversational dialogue with either believers or unbelievers. There are undoubtedly several reasons why this

---

[30]The word *dialegomai* is used 10 times in the book of Acts to describe Paul's ministry - Acts 17:2 & 17; 18:4 & 19; 19:8 & 9, 20:7 & 9; 24:25). The word *euangelidzo* appears 7 times in Paul's ministry in Acts (13:23; 14:7, 15, 21; 15:35; 16:10 & 17:18) and the word *kerusso* appears 2 times in Paul's Acts ministry(Acts 20:25 & 28:31).

## Teaching, Preaching and Talking

has happened, including the poor example we have been given by leaders who prefer to preach at unbelievers rather than engaging in a reasoned conversation with them. There's always more excitement in putting on a show for a large audience than there is in carrying on a reasoned conversation with a few people.

Perhaps another reason for our inability to engage in a genuine conversational dialogue with other people is the fear of our own ignorance. For example, if you don't really know or understand what you believe or why you believe it, it is difficult to carry on a prolonged or in-depth conversation with someone whose questions are anything more than superficial.

Finally, our own pride can get in the way of a conversation. I have watched far too many Christians communicate an air of *"I really do know more than you do, so you should be quiet and just listen to me"* when communicating

> *"House Churches are not particularly conducive to eloquent preaching, and not everyone can preach eloquently."*

with both unbelievers and their fellow believers. And when it comes to pride, eloquent and passionate preaching tends to exalt the messenger. And Christians love looking good on YouTube, even at the expense of being effective.

House churches are not particularly conducive to eloquent preaching, and not everyone can preach eloquently. But organic house churches can be a safe place where people with questions and problems can enter into a reasoned discussion, regarding the questions and issues confronting them in their search for Christ, or in their search for a more fulfilling and informed walk with Him. We need to learn how to say, *"Let's talk about that."*

**Remember:** Religious people often struggle with the idea of a dialogue because of their inability to control the discussion or its outcome. As a result they will often try to dominate the discussion.

**Reflection Question # 1 -** What have you learned about teaching, preaching and discussing in this Chapter that you did not know before?

**Reflection Question # 2 -** Reflecting on the difference between *affective* and *cognitive* learning, discuss a time in your spiritual life when a profound experience (*affective*) forced you to re-examine what you had been taught (*cognitive*) in order to find a biblical answer.

**Reflection Question # 3 -** Which do you think is the greater need among Christians today: To be roused or to be taught? Why?

**Reflection Question # 4 -** What are some ways you and your house church can engage in a genuine dialogue (i.e., a reasoned discussion) about spiritual truths you are experiencing as a house church?

# Chapter 15

## Beware The Wanderers

*Planet:* plan·et \pla-nət\ *Middle English planete, from Anglo-French, from Late Latin* <u>planeta</u>*, modification of Greek* <u>planēt-</u>*,* <u>planēs</u>*, literally, wanderer, from* <u>planasthai</u> *to wander.*

Like most ancient civilizations, the Greeks were astute students of the night sky. They studied the stars, mapped the constellations and learned to tell time and discern the changing seasons by changes in the heavens. One of the things they quickly noticed was that, whereas the stars

> *"False teachers were simply teachers who 'wandered' away from sound teaching, and who caused others to wander as well."*

were constant in their positions and movements, there were other objects which seemed to wander in the night sky. They called these night-time wanderers *planēs* - "planets." The Greek word group conveyed the idea of *"wandering,"* and then *"to lead astray"* or *"to go astray."* While the original sense and usage was of a literal wandering (like planets in the night sky), over time the word group came to be applied to the moral and spiritual spheres as well, being used to describe *"one who leads astray."* False teachers were simply teachers who wandered away from sound teaching, and who caused others to wander as well. In the New Testament the word group is used to describe both the deception and those who deceive. In other words: false teachers and their teaching. A false teacher is a deceiver, someone who wanders away, and causes others to wander away, from the truth of the faith. Doctrinal error is simply that teaching which results from having wandered away from *"the faith which was once for all delivered to the saints"* (Jude 1:3). And false teachers are teachers who cause their listeners to wander. This was true in the house churches of the New Testament. How do we know? Because Jude tells us so:

*"Beloved, while I was making every effort to write you about our common salvation, I felt the necessity to write to you appealing that you contend earnestly for the faith which was once for all delivered to the saints. For certain persons have crept in unnoticed . . ."* (Jude 1:3-4).

The rest is window dressing. You get the point. It was true then. It is true in churches today. It is true, or soon will be, in your house church. Are you prepared to deal with it?

### Whatever Happened to The Main Thing?

Times change. People don't. The constant over time is human nature, which explains why Paul's (and Jude's) admonitions to the house churches of the New Testament are as valid today as they were when he gave them (under the inspiration of the Holy Spirit) some 2,000 years ago.

If there is a difference today, twenty-one centuries later, it is that our Postmodern culture in the West has made the search for truth "ego-centric." In other words, truth really is all about "me." Personal opinions, regardless of how outlandish, have become self-authenticating and self-validating. My

# Beware The Wanderers

opinions are true because I hold them, because I believe them to be true, or if you're **really** spiritual, they're true because *"the Lord revealed it to me."* And, after all, who can argue with "the BIG dog."

From personal opinion (or personal revelation) we quickly move to what Walter Truett Anderson calls *"Socially Constructed Realities."*[31] This means we gather around us like-minded (or similarly deceived) people who

*". . . our Postmodern culture in the West has made the search for truth 'ego-centric.' In other words, truth really is all about 'me'."*

agree with us and create our own social network based upon a common belief. Or, alternatively, we go looking for a wandering teacher who agrees with us. In the age of the internet, this is easier than ever. Want to believe that you're one of the end-time Manifest Sons of God? There's a website for that (actually, more than one). Want to believe that everyone will eventually be saved and that *"All Dogs Go To Heaven"*?[32] I can give you several websites for that one. Want to believe that Jesus returned in 70 AD and that we're now living in the new heavens and the new earth? Yep, there's a website for that, too. Want to believe that Jesus loves you more if you keep the Old Testament dietary laws?

---

[31]Walter Truett Anderson, **Reality Isn't What It Used to Be** (San Francisco: Harper and Row, 1990).

[32]O.K., shameless plug for my book, **All Dogs Go To Heaven, Don't They: Biblical Reflections on Christian Universalism and Ultimate Reconciliation,** available on our website from Amazon.com.

## Safe Houses of Hope And Prayer

Yep, websites, teachers and books galore on that one (even a whole denomination!). In fact, give me your theologically aberrant (a transliteration of the Latin verb _aberrare_, meaning _"to go astray, to wander"_) view and I can probably find you a teacher, a website, a book and a ministry which all agree with you. That's the age in which we live. Proving, again, the wisdom of the ol' hymn writer who opined, _"Prone to wander, Lord, I feel it; prone to leave the God I love."_

O.K., I have a basic question: Whatever happened _to "the main thing"_? Remember this quote from our earlier book: _"The main thing is to always remember to keep the main thing the main thing."_ So, what exactly is _"the main thing"_? Author and Missiologist Alan Hirsch says that the early Church summarized _"the main thing"_ in a simple, "sneezable" declaration: _"Jesus is Lord."_ For the next 250 years this declaration of Christian faith was truly revolutionary as it stood in clear contradistinction to the prevailing Caesar worship of the Roman Empire which demanded that every good Roman declare that _"Caesar is Lord."_ They really didn't care what you believed, so long as you understood who the top dog was.

> _"The health and viability of any church . . . . can be measured by the extent to which it either remains true to or wanders away from 'the main thing'."_

To summarize it in terms for today, _"the main thing"_ is that set of core beliefs or tenants of faith which lie at the heart of the New Testament. It is Jesus, crucified, risen, coming again. And it is that message which He both embodied and proclaimed: _"The Kingdom of God is at hand; repent and_

## Beware The Wanderers

*believe the good news."* The health and viability of any church, including the church which meets in your house, can be measured by the extent to which it either remains true to or wanders away from *"the main thing."*

Ask yourself this simple question: If a complete stranger were to visit your house church gathering, when they left to go home what would they conclude was "the main thing" in your meeting? If it is anything other than Jesus and the Kingdom of God, you have a potentially serious problem.

> *"The Church of the 21st Century, including the organic house church movement, is in a contest for sound doctrine."*

### The Contest For Sound Doctrine

Make no mistake about it. The Church of the 21st Century, including the organic house church movement, is in a contest for sound doctrine. Doctrine rightly interpreted, clearly taught and authentically lived out before a watching, skeptical world. We find ourselves today in the same place Paul warned Timothy about when he said,

*"I charge you in the presence of God and of Christ Jesus, who is to judge the living and the dead, and by his appearing and his kingdom: preach the word; be ready in season and out of season; reprove, rebuke, and exhort, with complete patience and teaching. For the time is coming when people will not endure sound teaching, but having itching ears they will accumulate for themselves teachers to suit their own passions, and will turn away from listening to the truth and*

*wander off into myths."* (2 Timothy 4:1-4)

As I read this passage I was so struck by the Greek text, particularly in verses 3-4 that I decided to do my own translation which better expresses the literal sense of the Greek:

Maurice's Literal Translation: *"For there will be a season when they will not put up with sound teaching, BUT according to their own desires, to themselves they will gather teachers who make the hearing itch, and on the one hand they will turn away from hearing the truth, and on the other hand they will turn aside to myths."*

Let me make four personal observations based upon this text, observations which I think are relevant to the place in which we find ourselves today as regards sound doctrine.

***Observation # 1: Bad Moon Rising.*** My apologies to John Fogerty and Credence Clearwater Revival, but bad doctrine - like bad moons - does seem to come in seasons (*kairos*). Things will be going along fine with no issues, then there will suddenly be a wave - an outbreak - of spiritual foolishness and bad doctrine from new people

*". . . people would rather believe error, regardless of how foolish it appears, than believe the truth, regardless of how clearly we teach it."*

wanting to share some new truth or experience they've encountered. Don't ask me why, 'cuz I don't know. But Scripture warns us to look out for it, and the experience of the Church throughout history seems to bear this out. Personally, I think we are now in one of those seasons when people would rather believe error, regardless of how foolish it appears, than believe the truth, regardless of how clearly we teach it.

This season reminds me of the joke about the man who thought he was dead. His wife took him to the doctor in the hope that the doctor could convince the man that he wasn't really dead. But try as he might the doctor couldn't convince the man that he wasn't dead. Finally he had an idea. He took the man to the hospital morgue. He pulled out the body of a dead man, took a scalpel and slit the dead man's wrist. No blood. He did this several times with several dead bodies and with the same result. No blood. He then turned to the man and said, *"Now, do you understand? Dead men don't bleed."* The man reluctantly agreed, whereupon the doctor grabbed the man's wrist and sliced it open, causing him to bleed profusely. The startled man looked a the doctor and exclaimed, *"O my gosh! Dead men **do** bleed!"* Welcome to the task and the challenge of teaching sound doctrine to professing believers in our Postmodern age, an age which seems to believe that dead men **do** bleed.

*Observation # 2: It's A Pain In The "Patoot."* In seasons such as the one we are in, people are not willing to put up with ("endure") sound doctrine.[33] Why? Because doing so is painful to their agenda. People unwilling to put up with sound

---

[33]The Greek verb *anecho* has a long history of meaning *"to hold or lift up, to prop, sustain or maintain,"* hence, *"to endure"* or *"to put up with."* These are all uses, whether literal or metaphorical, which require effort.

doctrine usually respond in one of two basic ways. The *first* way they respond is to stumble over what they regard as the hard doctrines of the faith, doctrines such as conscious eternal punishment (hell).[34] People who stumble over such doctrines soon begin questioning and jettisoning other beliefs as well. The *second* way people respond is to simply get bored with basic sound doctrine and go *"a wanderin'"* in search of novel beliefs or new experiences. They will go chasing after gemstones or gold dust or angelic manifestations or whatever the latest spiritual fad might be. Why? Because the basics are boring and upholding them is hard work.

*Observation # 3: I Want What I Want!* People have a tendency to follow their own desires. In other words, people who wander away from "the main thing" during the seasons we're describing aren't so much on a personal search for

> *"(People) want what they want **more** than they want truth and sound doctrine."*

truth as they are on a personal search for teachers and teachings which agree with their desires. Simply put, they want what they want *more* than they want truth and sound doctrine. If you want unusual manifestations, you'll go looking for them. For this reason alone, be careful what you want. You'll probably find it.

---

[34]I deal with the problem of "hard" doctrines in my refutation of Universalism. See Chapter 8 of our book, *All Dogs Go To Heaven, Don't They: Biblical Reflections on Christian Universalism and Ultimate Reconciliation*, available on our website from Amazon.com.

# Beware The Wanderers

***Observation # 4: "Finally, Someone Who Agrees With Me!"*** People who want what they want will eventually find teachers who will give them what they want, and who will not only scratch their itch, but will give them NEW itches (which, of course, only they can scratch). Be warned: God's judgment and chastisement in our lives is sometimes to give us the very thing we want.

Finally, whether consciously or unconsciously, people make two fundamental choices. First, they choose to turn away from the truth. They may do this for any

> *"God's judgment and chastisement in our lives is sometimes to give us the very thing we want."*

wide variety of reasons (whether personal or philosophical), but at the end of the day they make a choice. And second, people choose to follow myths (see 1 Timothy 1:4 and Titus 1:14). Beware the choices you make.

***Observation # 5: False Prophets Versus False Teachers.*** When we step back from the Scriptures and focus on the big picture what we should quickly see is that false teachers are to the New Testament what false prophets were to the Old Testament (See 2 Peter 2:1 where Peter draws this comparison). The prophet

> *". . . false teachers are to the New Testament what false prophets were to the Old Testament."*

in the Old Testament carried the authority of bringing the word of God to the people of God. In the New Testament, it is the teacher who brings God's word to His people and

195

thereby exercises a higher degree of authority. And just as the prophet in the Old Testament was held to a higher standard of accountability because of the authority he wielded, so too, the teacher in the New Testament is held to a higher standard of accountability, as James reminds us: *"Let not many of you become teachers, my brethren, knowing that as such we will incur a stricter judgment."* (James 3:1) This explains why there are more warnings against false teachers in the New Testament than against false prophets.

## An Explicit Word From The Holy Spirit

*"But the Spirit explicitly says that in later times some will fall away from the faith, paying attention to deceitful spirits and doctrines of demons . . ."* (1 Timothy 4:1, NASB)

Want to have some fun? The next time someone asks you for an explicit "word from the Lord" give them this one! It doesn't get any more explicit than this! Once again, as in the previous passage, Paul warns us that there will come a time (again, *kairos* - season) when people will fall away from the faith because they paid attention to deceitful (*planēs*) spirits. This tells me several important things.

*First,* it tells me that you and I need to be very careful who and what we listen to. We live in a time when we need to put a premium on discernment.

*Second*, this passage warns me that there are spiritual entities (demons) afoot in both the world and the church which are dedicated to causing us to wander away from the faith. People wander from the truth for two basic causes: 1) because they make a personal choice to wander, and 2) because they are helped (pushed, enticed, etc.) by demonic entities who specialize in getting people to wander. In short, this is both a personal battle and a spiritual battle.

**Third,** there are demonic doctrines afoot in the church, doctrines inspired by Satan himself which need to be identified, refuted and avoided. Let's be clear. Beelzebub is a *"theologian extraordinaire."* Or as A. W. Tozer once observed, *"The devil is a better theologian than any of us, and is a devil still."*[35]

### Three "Smell Tests" Of A Genuine Word

*"For our appeal does not spring from error (planēs) or impurity or any attempt to deceive (dolos), but just as we have been approved by God to be entrusted with the gospel, so we speak, not to please man, but to please God who tests our hearts."* (1 Thessalonians 2:3-4)

In this passage I think Paul gives the Thessalonian believers (and us) three basic "smell tests" of a genuine message, teaching, prophecy or exhortation:

**Smell Test #1:** Does the message being delivered cause people to wander away from the basic truths of the faith? Is this teaching leading people away from *"the main thing"*?

**Smell Test #2:** Is the message being delivered spiritually

---

[35]A. W. Tozer, **Man - The Dwelling Place of God** (Fig Books, 2013). See *"Chapter 16 - On Taking Too Much For Granted."*

"unclean"? The Greek word here (*akatharsia*) is frequently used of moral impurity. If you've never encountered an "unclean spirit" in the church then you haven't gotten around much. I am no expert in this area, just an amateur with 40 years of practice. But from my study of Scripture and my experience in the church I have found these gnarly little buggers to be the spiritual motivation behind a wide variety of activities, including but not limited to moral impurity. I have been in gatherings and teaching meetings where the use (and overuse) of sexual imagery was downright disturbing. But the work of unclean spirits is also manifested in other works of the flesh including fear, woundedness, anger, bitterness, and false prophecy.

**Smell Test #3:** Is the message deceitful? The word *"to deceive"* in verse 3 is the Greek word *dolos*. In Classical times this word referred to *"any cunning contrivance for deceiving or catching"* and was used to describe the infamous Trojan Horse. This is where discernment becomes important. Is a teacher being deceitful? Is he or she using rhetorical slight of hand (a cunning contrivance) to bring listeners to a wrong conclusion? Is the word or argument being presented a trick to lead people astray through a subtle misrepresentation or misinterpretation of Scripture? In other words, is it deceitful, with the result of being unclean and causing people to wander from the basics of the faith?

## Suggestions For Your House Church

*1. Be on the lookout.* Be on the look out for wanderers in your fellowship. It is the calling of elders, in their function as shepherds, to continually be on the lookout for threats to the

## Beware The Wanderers

spiritual health of the flock. And wandering people and wandering spirits are one such threat. If you don't believe that, then the New Testament is meaningless. It's all there in pretty clear language. Your house church may be the exception to the New Testament rule, but I doubt it.

**2. Get clean.** I've started getting phone calls from believers who have been hopping from place to place and their comments are enlightening: *"I'm tired of the weirdness that I'm finding out there. I'm looking for a clean fellowship that just wants to seek the Lord. Can I come to your group?"*

So, how do you get spiritually clean? **First,** learn to nip wandering nonsense in the bud early, not later. The longer it goes, the harder it is to confront. **Second,** learn to spend prolonged time together as a body in worship and waiting upon God. The length of time you as a body can sit in silent prayer and worship before the throne is often an indicator of the weirdness level in your group. Spiritual weirdness often has difficulty with silence and quickly wants to fill it - often with a lot of self-proclamation nonsense, or binding the heavenlies or strategic spiritual warfare or other nonsense that sounds spiritual but isn't.

> *"The length of time you as a body can sit in silent prayer and worship before the throne is often an indicator of the 'weirdness level' in your group."*

**Third,** listen to what God is saying to His Church for these times. As I have shared both in this book and in our previous book, **River Houses Rising**, we received a **very** clear word that God intends to do three things among His Church in these times: 1) He intends to return a powerful sense of holiness and the fear of God to His people; 2) He intends to return a powerful spirit of repentance to His Church; and 3) He intends to instil a greater sense of intimacy with His Church. If you want to get "spiritually clean" as an organic house church, spend time worshiping God together and pursuing those three things in prayer.[36]

***3. Recover your theological roots.*** We live in a Postmodern age where it is fashionable to question everything, including everything the church has traditionally taught. While this can sound "chic" and spiritual, there is a huge unspoken danger here.

> *". . . in order to destroy a people you must first sever their roots."*

The Russian dissident and Nobel prize winning novelist, Alexander Solzhenitsyn, once observed that in order to destroy a people you must first sever their roots. We live in an age of severed roots, both inside and outside the church. And a rootless church (like a rootless believer) is one subject to every wind of false doctrine that blows.

But at the end of the day, everyone has a theology, a dogma, if you will. Do you know what yours is? If not, Beelzebub, that

---

[36]We discuss this in detail in our book, **The Inextinguishable Blaze: God's Call to Holiness, Repentance, Intimacy and Spiritual Awakening**, available on our website from Amazon.com. See particularly *"Chapter 4 - What The Angels Said."*

# Beware The Wanderers

*"theologian extraordinaire"* will eat you for lunch. I'm already working with house church people who have experienced this. Don't let it happen to you. Drive some theological stakes in the ground for yourself and your house church. If you need help, get a good introduction to historic Christian doctrine as well as a basic systematic theology, and make these your reference points.[37] The discipline of thinking systematically alone will be beneficial in helping you work through theological issues when they arise.

***Reflection Question # 1 -*** What have you learned about false teachers and false teaching in this Chapter that you did not know before?

***Reflection Question # 2 -*** What is the point of similarity between false prophets in the Old Testament and false teachers in the New Testament?

***Reflection Question # 3 -*** What are some practical steps you and your house church can take to exercise discernment and avoid and combat false teachers?

---

[37]Two that I recommend are J. I. Packer, ***Concise Theology: A Guide to Historic Christian Beliefs*** (Carol Stream, Il: Tyndale House Publishers, Inc., 2001), and Wayne Grudem, ***Systematic Theology: An Introduction to Biblical Doctrine*** (Grand Rapids: Zondervan, 1994).

# Safe Houses of Hope And Prayer

# Chapter 16

## Biblical Community

### The Greatest StarTrek Episode Ever Made

#### Let Me Help

It is known as the penultimate StarTrek episode, simply the best episode ever made. To StarTrek afficionados it is known as *Season One, Episode 28, airdate April 6, 1967.* To collectors of the boxed DVD set it is known as *"The City On The Edge Of Forever."*

While the Enterprise is investigating temporal disturbances from a nearby planet, Mr. Sulu is injured by a shock wave and explosion. Dr. McCoy gives Sulu a shot of cordrazine which saves his life. But when another shock wave rocks the Enterprise, Dr. McCoy accidentally injects himself with an overdose, rendering him delusional. He flees from the Bridge to the Transporter Room and beams himself down to the planet. Kirk and a landing party beam down to the planet surface where they find both Dr. McCoy and  the source of the time distortions. An ancient glowing ring  located among ageless ruins speaks and introduces itself and the *"Guardian of Forever,"* a gateway to other times and places. Escaping the clutches of the distracted landing party, McCoy jumps through the portal. Suddenly the landing party loses contact with the Enterprise. The Guardian explains that the past has been altered and the Enterprise no longer exists. In order to repair the timeline, Kirk and Spock must use the Guardian to go in search of  McCoy.

# Safe Houses of Hope And Prayer

Passing through the Guardian, Kirk and Spock arrive in New York City during the Great Depression of the 1930s. After stealing some clothes to blend in, and running from the Police, they take refuge in the 21st Street Rescue Mission run by a woman named Edith Keeler (played by Joan Collins). They go to work for Ms. Keeler, who knows theses two are different, but doesn't know why or how. Spock devotes his time and energy to building a computer *"out of stone knives and bear skins"* in order to read information stored on his tricorder which might explain what McCoy has done to alter history. Kirk begins to fall in love with Edith, whom he finds remarkable. On an evening stroll together, Edith expresses her desire to help Kirk with whatever trouble he may be in. *"Let me help,"* she implores. Kirk responds by pointing Edith to a star on Orion's belt and telling her that a 100 years from then an author from a planet circling that star will write a best selling book based upon those three words, *"Let Me Help,"* even recommending them over *"I love you."* There's more to the episode, but I'll leave it to you to find a copy on Netflix and watch for yourself.

## The "Let Me Help" of Biblical Community

By now you should be asking yourself, *"How in the name of Star Fleet is he going to tie this together?"* Thanks. I was hoping you would ask. The New Testament actually has a lot to say on the topic of *"Let Me Help."* It simply expresses it in different language.

**First,** as we saw earlier in Chapter 8, the New Testament approach to *"Let Me Help"* begins with those individuals whom God has gifted as leaders in the Church, specifically

# Biblical Community

the itinerant 5-Fold leadership gifts: Apostles, Prophets, Evangelists, Pastors and Teachers (described in Ephesians 4:11-16). With every gift comes a responsibility. The calling and responsibility of

> *"The stress of life and ministry in this present evil age shreds our nets, sometimes beyond our ability to mend them without help."*

the 5-Fold ministry gift is to help by equipping believers for the work of service (Eph. 4:12). As we have previously see, the Greek word translated *"equip"* is _katartidzo_, meaning *"to render (something) fit."* It is used in Matthew 4:21-22 & Mark 1:19-20 to describe the disciples mending their nets. I like to describe the role of the 5-Fold leadership gifts as teaching the church *"the fine art of mending one another's nets."*

Let's face reality for a moment, shall we. The stress of life and ministry in this present evil age shreds our nets, sometimes beyond our ability to mend them without help, producing the messiness of life both inside and outside of the _ekklesia_. The calling of the 5-fold gifts is to come alongside the Church - both individually and corporately - and to say, *"Let me help. I see your nets are torn in this area. Let me help you mend them."*

**Second,** the New Testament approach to *"Let Me Help"* is expressed in what I call the *"One Anothers"* of biblical community. I believe that one of the roles of 5-fold leaders is to be the tuning fork of the Church. The set the tone of *"Let Me Help,"* a tone which then resonates throughout the community of believers. But the real work of building biblical community is expressed in the *"One Anothers"* of the New

# Safe Houses of Hope And Prayer

Testament.

Throughout the New Testament we find commands expressly given to the Church regarding how believers are to behave toward *"one another."* I have found more than 30 of them. The most famous and most repeated *"One Another"* is the admonition to *"love one another,"* which occurs some 20 times. Here is a sample of a dozen *"One Anothers"* (remember, there are 25 more where these came from!):

1. Love One Another
2. Be Devoted To One Another
3. Live In Harmony With One Another
4. Welcome One Another
5. Give Preference To One Another
6. Be of The Same Mind Toward One Another
7. Owe Nothing To One Another
8. Do Not Judge One Another
9. Build Up One Another
10. Accept One Another
11. Admonish One Another
12. Serve One Another

Quite frankly, these sound very churchy, even down right platitudinal. A platitude is *"a remark or statement, especially one with a moral content, that has been used too often to be interesting or thoughtful."* Another definition says a platitude is *"a flat, dull, or trite remark, especially one uttered as if it were fresh or profound."* Sound familiar? It should. That's exactly how most believers treat the *"One Anothers"* of Scripture. We've heard them so often that they no longer interest or challenge us. They have become trite and dull. And that goes a long way toward explaining why we have so

# Biblical Community

little genuine biblical community in church.

But what if we were to take a cue from StarTrek? What if we were to think of the *"One Anothers"* of Scripture in the personalized terms of *"Let Me Help."* Then the *"One Anothers"* of Scripture might look and sound a bit more interesting, not to mention more personally challenging:

1.  Let Me Love You
2.  Let me Be Devoted To You
3.  Let Me Live In Harmony With You
4.  Let Me Welcome You Into My Home And My Life
5.  Let Me Prefer You Over Others
6.  Let Me Be of One Mind With You
7.  Let Me Owe You Nothing But Love (And Absolve You Of Any Debt To Me)
8.  Let Me Not Judge You
9.  Let Me Build You Up
10. Let Accept You For Who You Are
11. Let Me Admonish You
12. Let Me Serve You

Sound better? The *"One Anothers"* of biblical community (or perhaps we should call them the *"Let Me Helps"* of biblical community) are, first and foremost, personal admonitions, guiding individual believers in how we are to act toward other fellow believers. Expressed this way, the *"Let Me Helps"* of biblical community are almost embarrassingly personal. They are so personal, in fact, that it is difficult to see how genuine biblical community can exist and thrive among believers in groups larger than 15-to-20 people, or about the maximum size of an organic house church.

# Safe Houses of Hope And Prayer

Think about it. Just how many people can you meaningfully love, or be devoted to, or live in harmony with, or welcome into your home and life, or be of one mind with, or build up, or admonish, or

> *". . . it is difficult to see how genuine biblical community can exist and thrive among believers in groups larger than 15-to-20 people."*

serve, etc.? Yes, we can preach these values and behaviors to a megachurch of 25,000 people, or to an average size American church of 360 people, but the personal and practical nature of their real-life application requires a relatively small group of 15-to-20 believers. If we need proof of this reality, we shouldn't need to look further than the example of Jesus. All of these *"One Anothers"* can be seen at work in His ministry to His twelve disciples. And I should add at this point that these *"Let Me Helps"* are given specifically to believers to guide their relationships with other believers. These are the values of life in the Kingdom given to guide disciples of the Kingdom in their life with one another. Their application toward unbelievers is secondary, if not tangential. If we can't get it right within the Church, what hope do we have of manifesting it to unbelievers in any meaningful way?

Welcome to the *"Let Me Help"* of biblical community and organic house church. I'll bet you never imagined that being a "Trekkie" could be so biblical.

# Biblical Community

## Reflection Question

Below I have listed thirty-six *"One Anothers"* from the New Testament, restated in the format of *"Let Me Help."* Reflect on how you might apply these in relationships within your own organic house church:

13.  Let Me Love You
14.  Let me Be Devoted To You
15.  Let Me Live In Harmony With You
16.  Let Me Welcome You Into My Home And My Life
17.  Let Me Prefer You Over Others
18.  Let Me Be of One Mind With You
19.  Let Me Owe You Nothing But Love (And Absolve You Of Any Debt To Me)
20.  Let Me Not Judge You
21.  Let Me Build You Up
22.  Let Accept You For Who You Are
23.  Let Me Admonish You
24.  Let Me Serve You
25.  Let Me Not Bite, Devour And Consume You
26.  Let Me Not Boast, Challenge And Envy You
27.  Let Me Show Forbearance Toward You
28.  Let Me Bear Your Burdens
29.  Let Me Be Kind To You
30.  Let Me Speak Spiritual Encouragement To You
31.  Let Me Be Subject To You
32.  Let Me Regard You
33.  Let Me Not Lie To You
34.  Let Me Bear With You
35.  Let Me Forgive You (And Ask Your Forgiveness As Well)

## Safe Houses of Hope And Prayer

36.     Let Me Teach You (And Learn From You)
37.     Let Me Comfort You
38.     Let Me Encourage You (And Be Encouraged In The Process)
39.     Let Me Stimulate You To Greater Love And Good Deeds
40.     Let Me Live In Peace With You
41.     Let Me Seek After That Which Is Good For You
42.     Let Me Not Speak Against You
43.     Let Me Not Complain Against You
44.     Let Me Confess My Failures To You
45.     Let Me Pray For You
46.     Let Me Be Hospitable To You
47.     Let Me Clothe Myself With Humility Toward You
48.     Let Me Wash Your Feet

# Chapter 17

## If I Had Organic House Church To Do Over Again

### Background

Consider this Chapter a retrospective. My wife and I have been involved in organic house church for nearly 15 years, after several fruitful years in a Presbyterian church and a stint as an interim pastor. My first organic church conference was with 75 people in Denver, Colorado organized by John White and a relatively new group called House2House. There I met Wolfgang Simson, Tony And Felicity Dale and others who have become known leaders in the organic house church movement over the years, and people I have been privileged to call friends and mentors. Over the years we've done radio programs, websites, newsletters, weekly gatherings, area-wide gatherings and more. Then, just as we were exploring the possibility of establishing an organic house church association, the Lord spoke to us very clearly and said, *"Lay it all down and walk away."* Yep, didn't really see that one coming.

What followed was a profound journey of laying down tightly-held ideas and plans combined with a season of care-taking two elderly parents while reflecting and writing on what we learned from more than a decade of organic church experiences. I want to share a few of these lessons with you.

We are committed organic church people. We've been ruined

for life by organic church. Organic church has become a value for us, as opposed to an alternative structure. At the heart of that value is an understanding that we don't go to church, rather, we are the church wherever we happen to be. For this reason alone, organic house church is immensely flexible. Theoretically speaking, there is no building to sell, no staff to fire, no programs to cancel, no overhead to cut. Simply put, the flexibility of organic church means that you and I always have the opportunity to do organic church over again. So, let's get started.

**If Jesus Led Your House Church**

Let's pretend for just a moment that Jesus showed up and announced that He was going to lead your house church. What do you think He would do? How much time do you think He would spend talking politics or end-time events, arguing

*"Like Bilbo Baggins, you might just find yourself on 'an unexpected journey' into discipleship and the Kingdom of God."*

over spiritual gifts or the role of women, or which praise CD we should use for worship? The late Michael Spencer once observed that Evangelical Christians want *"Jesus on the cover but not in the book."* In other words, Jesus sells well, but no one actually wants to take Him seriously. After all, let's face reality. If you turn Jesus loose in your church the probability is high that He will make a royal mess of things. He might just tell you (and me) to drop your nets, drop what you're currently doing, and *"Follow Me."* And who knows where that kind of invitation might lead. Like Bilbo Baggins, you might just find yourself on an unexpected journey into discipleship and the Kingdom of God.

At the end of the day, I believe Jesus would do the same thing today that He did two-thousand years ago. He would focus His time, attention and energy on making disciples. I believe Jesus would challenge our religion-shaped spirituality, just as He challenged the religion

*"Discipleship as Jesus practiced it is about accepting the yoke of obedience to the call of the Kingdom and following that yoke wherever He and it lead us."*

shaped spirituality of His first disciples. For the sake of world redemption, Jesus needed to free His disciples from the narrow religion-shaped spirituality given to them by 1st Century Judaism. In turn, He would replace it with a spirituality modeled upon Himself. What religion-shaped spirituality would He want to replace in your organic house church? If you don't think you have one, I'll be glad to lend you a mirror. Really.

Discipleship as Jesus practiced it is about accepting the yoke of obedience to the call of the Kingdom and following that yoke wherever He and it lead us. Jesus yoked His disciples to Himself, and refused to release them until their religion-shaped spirituality had given way and been replaced with a Jesus-shaped spirituality. Jesus challenged their understanding of religion until He embodied their understanding of religion. He challenged their understanding of spirituality until He embodied their understanding of spirituality. And He challenged their understanding of the

Kingdom of God until He, and He alone, embodied their understanding of the Kingdom. And that is how He wants to challenge and transform each of us today. He wants to challenge our understanding of discipleship until He embodies our understanding of discipleship. That, I believe, is what Jesus would do if He were here to lead our house churches today. If we respond by saying, *"Well, we believe Jesus IS here among us today to lead our house churches,"* then we are confronted with a profoundly disturbing question: *"Why aren't we doing what we know Jesus would do? Why aren't we making disciples the way He did?"*

## Doing Organic House Church Over Again

So, let's return to what all of this means for doing organic house church differently. If I had organic house church to do over again (and I do!), here is my short list of what I would do.

The first thing I would do is to stop doing nearly everything we have been doing. Yes, even if it means being being accused (falsely) of forsaking assembling together. Some things need to be forsaken. If that means cancelling meetings and telling people *"We're done"* for a season, that's what I would do. Why? Because, we need to take the time to re-evaluate and re-boot what we are doing.

Those of us who have been involved in organic house church for a while like to say that *"Jesus wants His Church back."* It's a catchy turn-of-phrase and I've used it more times than I can remember. So have you. The problem is that, in spite of all

# If I Had Organic Church To Do Over

our talk, Jesus hasn't gotten his Church back. Far too often what Jesus has gotten back is a group of well-intentioned believers practicing the same religious habits they learned in traditional church, but now they're

*"Jesus wants to make disciples of the Kingdom willing to walk in radical faith and radical obedience, to walk with Him, to worship Him and to obey Him."*

doing it in someone's living room. Soon, old agendas, left over from the last thing we were involved with, re-emerge and organic church has become re-agendized. Organic church is now all about (check your favorite): missions, spiritual gifts, worship, teaching, church planting, etc.). Welcome to agendized organic church.

I have slowly come to the conclusion that Jesus, too, has an agenda for organic church. Jesus wants to make disciples of the Kingdom willing to walk in radical faith and radical obedience, to walk with Him, to worship Him and to obey Him. That's Jesus' agenda for His Church, regardless of where it meets. For this reason alone, if I had organic church to do over again (and, thankfully, I do) I would make discipleship the heart and soul of everything we do. I would focus on a relatively small group of 8-to-12 people. Together we would examine and embrace the same discipleship lessons and Kingdom values which Jesus taught His disciples.

Today we have too many professing believers who demonstrate little or no interest in being disciples of Jesus and the Kingdom, at least not on Jesus' terms. They are free range believers who want Jesus on the cover of what they do, but not in the book. Nor do they have any interest in making disciples on Jesus' terms. If people aren't interested in discovering what it means to be a disciple of

> *"Jesus wasn't looking for followers, or 'believers,' or even 'laborers' . . . . He was looking for disciples."*

the Kingdom and to make disciples of the Kingdom, then it's time to let them go on their way. There's probably a fine ministry meeting, conference center or church somewhere in town where the worship music is snappy, the message is short, they have child-care and a bistro and they can do their own thing as free range believers with minimal commitment. While that may seem harsh, it isn't. It's what Jesus did. He discipled twelve, trained another seventy-two, and sent thousands of believers and would-be followers home. Why? Because Jesus wasn't looking for followers, or believers or even laborers (I believe Jesus used concept of laborers as a metaphor for disciples, just as He used wheat and harvest as metaphors for the unsaved masses). He was looking for disciples. What are we looking for?

Let's reflect for a moment. Jesus' challenge and task on earth was profoundly simple. In a span of three years He must impart to a handful of individuals sufficient eternal truth to transform their lives and to carry the message of the Kingdom and a growing Church forward until His return at the end of the Age. The method He chose to accomplish this task was elegantly simple. He would pick twelve unlikely individuals and spend the next three years pouring Himself into them. They would be His disciples, his *"padawan learners,"* if you will. In their company He would preach, teach and model everything they would need to know about

# If I Had Organic Church To Do Over

the Kingdom of God in order to carry His Church forward after He was gone. Discipleship was Jesus' plan and method for the Kingdom from now until His return. But is it our plan? Is that what we're doing?

This of course raises a question: What did Jesus teach those twelve disciples that so transformed their lives? What lessons did Jesus teach His disciples regarding the message, the ministry and the mission of the Kingdom of God. What did He teach them about the cost of discipleship and what it means to be a disciple of

*"Discipleship was Jesus' plan and method for the Kingdom from now until His return."*

that Kingdom? How exactly did Jesus challenge the religion-shaped spirituality of twelve 1st Century Jews in order to transform them into disciples of the Kingdom? Why did He repeat certain lessons, but not others? What did Jesus teach them about how the Kingdom of God challenges and changes our spiritual priorities? How many times did Jesus actually call the disciples (it's more than once, trust me!), and why the lapse of time between calls? What did Jesus teach the twelve about ministry to the marginalized, and how many times did He repeat the lesson? What did Jesus teach His disciples about the call, the lifestyle and the task of the Kingdom? And why have we not understood and taught those same lessons to those we seek to disciple? These are just a few of the discipleship questions and lessons I've personally been challenged by over the past year as I've studied the gospels and reflected on discipleship and the Kingdom of God. I've identified over seventy lessons Jesus intentionally taught His disciples.[38]

I have been encouraged lately as I have seen others re-examining the issue of discipleship. Authors such as David Platt (*Radical* and *Follow Me*) are challenging more people to think more about the meaning of discipleship. Discipleship is becoming a popular discussion topic among writers, bloggers and conference speakers. Hopefully, genuine discipleship will become more than another fad for conference goers, or another megachurch book-CD-Sermon-Curriculum-Program ("40 Days To Discipleship"). Time will tell.

At the age of 59, and having spent almost three years helping my wife care-take her elderly parents, I have been reminded of just how short our pilgrimage in this life really is. It is a sobering moment when you realize just how quickly eternity is approaching, and how true it is for each of us that *"night is coming when no man can work"* (John 9:4). My take-away lesson from this experience with respect to organic church and ministry is simple, yet personally profound. I don't have time to waste playing church anymore. Not even organic house church. And neither do you.

It is time to re-evaluate and re-boot. It's time to give Jesus His Church back, and in the process, to take on His yoke of discipleship and to pursue organic church and the Kingdom of God the way He originally taught His disciples to pursue it.

---

[38]See our book, ***And They Dreamt of A Kingdom,*** available on our website from Amazon.com.